Lawyerball

LAWYERBALL

The Courtroom Battle of the Orioles Against the Nationals and MLB for the Future of Baseball

CHARLES H. MARTIN

Acknowledgements

Quotations in Chapter 2 are taken from interviews with Ted Lerner, Ed Cohen, and Debra Cohen in the *Washingtonian* magazine article of June 1, 2007, "Ted Lerner Plays Ball" by Harry Jaffe, and used with the permission of *Washingtonian*.

Epigraphs in Chapters 3 and 9 are taken from *Wiktionary.org* and *Wikipedia.org*, and are licensed under Creative Commons at https://creativecommons.org/licenses/by-sa/3.0.

Epigraph in Chapter 5 is taken from *The Game: Inside the Secret World of Major League Baseball's Power Brokers* by Jon Pessah. Copyright © 2015 by Jon Pessah. Used by permission of Little, Brown and Company.

Copyright © 2016 Charles H. Martin

All rights reserved.

ISBN-10: 0-9896488-3-4
ISBN-13: 978-0-9896488-3-7

See more information related to this book at www.lawyerball.com

DEDICATION

For my grandfather, a Griffith Stadium vendor for more than thirty years, who told me he saw Babe Ruth hit a pop fly so high that "Ruth was standing on third base when the fielder missed it, and Ruth ran home for an inside-the-park homer."

For my father, who took me to many games at D.C./R.F.K. Stadium, where we watched the Senators lose.

For Wayne, Darryl and Butch, my sandlot baseball buddies.

INTRODUCTION

An owners' fight over an "inside baseball" arbitration splitting cable television profits spills into a New York City trial court. *Lawyerball* traces this dispute from the baseball antitrust exemption to the implications of the judge's rulings for the baseball business, the game, its fans, and ordinary Americans.

Lawyerball tells the story of the monopolization of baseball as an American business, and its disappearance from much of American life. It has lessons about the shrinking rights of Americans to go to court with their grievances. It also has lessons about the vanishing freedom of Americans to choose their work. This story about the future of baseball might foretell the future of America.

In 2005, thirty Major League Baseball clubs owned the near-bankrupt Montreal Expos. The clubs signed a television contract with the Baltimore Orioles. The Orioles owner agreed to not sue MLB over the relocation of the Expos to Washington, D.C. In return, MLB gave the Orioles the rights to cablecast the Washington Nationals future games. MLB then sold the Expos to a Washington real estate billionaire. He had to work with the Orioles owner, a class-action lawyer, to make a contract work that he had not negotiated.

The first time these owners were required to cooperate, accusations flew between them. Three years later, the Orioles, the Nationals and MLB sat before a New York trial judge. He would decide how to shift more than $100 million dollars between the teams. He would chart the future of baseball.

[Reader Alert - ...] I have added these alerts from page 78 to page 117 to connect relevant contract sections with later arguments in court. After all, I know where this story is headed. Shouldn't you know too?

TABLE OF CONTENTS

	Prologue	1
1	The First Inning – Senators, Twins, Expos, Nationals, Browns and Orioles	21
2	The Second Inning – Soldiers, Clerks, Steelmakers, Dealmakers and Litigators	43
3	The Third Inning – An Antitrust Exemption Creates a Major League Baseball Cartel	55
4	The Fourth Inning – Cable TV Builds and Internet Live-Streaming Rebuilds Baseball	83
5	The Fifth Inning – The Orioles and MLB Stick the Nationals With a One-Sided Cable Television Contract	97
6	The Sixth Inning – What Does That Clause Mean?	121
7	The Seventh Inning – The Rights Fees Dispute Goes Into Overtime	141
8	The Eighth Inning – The Judge Tries	155

To Figure It Out

9 The Ninth Inning – Contracts, Competition and the Lessons of Baseball   215

Bibliography   245

PROLOGUE

Mr. Applegate: "Would you like to be the greatest baseball player in all history?"

Joe Boyd/Joe Hardy: "Ha! Big joke."

Mr. Applegate: "No joke.... With my help a lot of things come easy.... The world is full of crazy things. Crazier everyday.... I have chosen you, the most dedicated partisan of the noble Washington Senators to be the hero who leads them out of the wilderness to the championship..."

Joe: "What happens after I stop being a baseball player. Then where would I be?"

Mr. Applegate: "Well now of course that's fairly well known.... After all there's nothing unusual about it. How do you suppose some of these politicians around town got started? And parking lot owners?....Look I've got something to trade here..."

Joe: "In my business we have what you call an escape clause."

Mr. Applegate: "This is not a real estate deal."

Joe: "If I don't like it, I ought to be able to get out."

Mr. Applegate: "Get out?.... Alright, I'll give you a chance to get out ... on the twenty-fourth of September at midnight. I wouldn't do it, but I don't want to have those damn Yankees win."

-from *Damn Yankees*, the Broadway musical/film

Copyright © George Abbott and Douglass Wallop, excerpted from the book of the play *Damn Yankees* and/or the screenplay of the 1958 film *Damn Yankees* and used here with express permission of the copyright owners. All Rights Reserved.

Baseball Goes To Court

60 Centre Street looms over Foley Square in downtown Manhattan like a Roman temple. It is the New York County state courthouse, where a line of legal supplicants waits for entrance through an X-ray and metal detector gauntlet on a gray May morning in 2015. High above these machines and the uniformed guards in the courthouse foyer, in the archway supporting the building dome, is a mural of two god-like figures with the titles "Protection" and "Security". Four gray-silver figures occupy the corners of the entrance vault. Their names are "Authority" (a man with a sword), "Justice" (a blindfolded woman with a sword), "Judgment" (a man with a book) and "Clemency" (a woman).

Men and women in blue and brown business suits enter a courtroom off the second floor rotunda balcony. Some walk with roll-a-bags carrying thick legal documents and files. The hands on the Roman numeral clock on the back wall are stuck on 12 and 8. In the fifteen-foot ceiling, recessed and pendant lights illuminate dark wood wainscoting. Chocolate brown seat pads cover wooden pews. The floor is dark brown with a black marble baseboard. Windows stretch from the tops of radiators to the ceiling. Window blinds cascade down to uncovered casements.

The courtroom is filling quickly for a hearing before Justice Lawrence Marks, of the New York County Supreme Court. Mid-Atlantic Sports Network (MASN) is a regional sports cable network that telecasts the games of the Baltimore Orioles and Washington Nationals baseball teams. Its majority owner has filed a motion that is the subject of the hearing.

A Major League Baseball (MLB) arbitration panel, composed of the owners of three other MLB teams, has required MASN to pay the Washington Nationals franchise (owned by the minority owner of MASN) an amount increasing from $53 million in 2012 to $66 million in 2016 for the rights to cablecast Nationals baseball games. Peter Angelos, the majority owner, wants to vacate the panel's decision.

The day of the hearing before Justice Marks is May 18, 2015.

Why Is the Orioles/MASN Lawsuit the Courtroom Battle for the Future of Baseball?

Why does this book describe this lawsuit as the courtroom battle for the future of baseball? Since 1922, when the U.S. Supreme Court exempted them from the antitrust laws of the United States, the "major leagues" have operated with few limitations on their power to grant or deny professional baseball franchises, to use anti-competitive practices against would-be competitors in the market for professional baseball, and to carve-up exclusive territories in which league "clubs" can operate without competition from other league "clubs".

This unique power has rarely been challenged in court. MLB owners avoid taking their disputes to public courts, where their league governance procedures and club finances might be exposed to public scrutiny. In the few cases where baseball's antitrust exemption has been challenged in court, federal appeals courts, and the U.S. Supreme Court itself, have said that the Supreme Court's 1922 decision was almost certainly wrong.

It had reasoned that professional baseball games were not subject to antitrust laws, because they were not "interstate commerce". Nevertheless, the Supreme Court has said that only the Congress should correct its mistake. Professional baseball has relied on this judicial antitrust exemption for so long, it says, that it would be unjust for that reliance to be penalized by a judicial overturning of the 1922 decision.

If successful, the lawsuit by the MASN regional sports channel against MLB to overturn its internal arbitration award to the Nationals could revolutionize professional baseball. All future decisions by MLB on revenue-sharing and other internal governance issues could become subject to oversight by federal judges as to the fairness and reasonableness of those decisions. The MLB cartel would, in effect, gain a board of directors composed of the more than eight hundred federal judges and several thousand state judges in the courts of the United States. This could be the worst of all worlds: a baseball cartel protected by the federal government and *run* by that government.

Four Pillars of The Baseball Business

The first recorded baseball game between organized teams occurred in Hoboken, New Jersey on June 19, 1846. The business of baseball, as we recognize it today, however, can be traced to five later milestones.

The Cincinnati Redstockings were organized in 1869 as the first team of professional baseball players. Men who played baseball for money joined and left various professional teams freely until 1879. In that year, the two-year old National League of Professional Base Ball Clubs addressed what some club owners perceived as the expensive problem of uncontrolled player mobility. Smaller city clubs complained that their best players were often lured away by the higher salary offers of bigger city clubs.

The First Pillar – The "Five Man Rule"

An unwritten arrangement was made in 1879. The owners agreed that none of them would bargain with a player on a list of five "reserved" players, who were under contract to play for another league team, without that team's permission. This prohibition applied even *after* the player's contract expired. By 1882, when the rival American Association of Base Ball Clubs was formed, this rule entered the National League Constitution.

The Second Pillar – The "National Agreement"

In 1883, all players on a team became subject to the "reserve clause". Under the terms of the "National Agreement for the Government of

Professional Base Ball Clubs" signed in that year, the National League, its "major league" competitor, the American Association of Professional Base Ball Clubs, and the "minor league" National Association of Professional Base Ball Leagues agreed to the reserve clause rules.

The Third Pillar – The Standard Player Contract "Reserve Clause"

In 1887, the reserve clause was written into all player contracts for the first time. A few valuable players objected to the reserve clause, like Providence's George Wright who said it "was outrageous, with no particle of justice in it." After winning fifty-nine games in 1884, Charley Radbourne said "The only difference between the league and slavery is that the managers can't lick you. They have you down so fine that you have no say in the matter at all. I sign a contract with a club, and they can hold me forever, if they see fit, or so long as I want to play ball."

The Fourth Pillar – The American League Joins the National Agreement

In 1903, after two years of player raids from the upstart American League of Professional Base Ball Clubs, the American League joined the National

Agreement, and agreed to respect its reserve clause rules. Arguments were made that the contract reserve clause was invalid, because contract law requires mutuality of obligations, also known as "consideration" from each party, in order for an agreement to be legally enforceable. Clubs could extend a player's one-year contract from year-to-year by exercising their unilateral option to do so. A player's only choice was to accept the extension, or to stop playing baseball. In 1912, this potential obstacle was addressed by an amendment to the National Agreement specifying that seventy-five percent of a player's salary was for his services in a particular year, and twenty-five percent was in return for the club's "right of reservation", the reserve clause.

From 1903 until 1975, the reserve clause, and the 1922 U.S. Supreme Court decision that rejected an antitrust challenge to it, established the foundation for a cartel of professional baseball clubs. The reserve clause was banned by the federal "Curt Flood Act" of 1998. The market for baseball players remained limited, however, by a series of collective bargaining labor agreements that the major leagues signed with the Major League Baseball Players Association, beginning in 1968.

The Creation and Reorganization of the Office of the Commissioner of Baseball

MLB was formed in 1999, through the merger of the offices of the National League and American League Commissioners into the single Office of the Commissioner of Major League Baseball. Previously, the league Commissioners had co-existed with the Commissioner of Baseball.

The first Commissioner of Baseball was Kenesaw Mountain Landis. Landis was an Illinois federal trial judge, who gained fame for his theatricality in court, and for fining Standard Oil $29,000,000 in a 1907 antitrust trial. Landis was chosen by the league owners to restore public confidence in the honesty of baseball after the "Black Sox" gambling scandal in the 1919 World Series.

Landis presided at the 1915 trial of *The Federal League of Professional Baseball Clubs vs. The National League of Professional Baseball Clubs* litigation, in which the Federal League alleged that the National and American Leagues used tactics that violated antitrust laws to force it out of business. The lawsuit was settled after the National League and American League owners reached various business accommodations with most of the Federal League owners. Only the owners of the Baltimore Terrapins club were dissatisfied with the settlement. These owners sued the major leagues for antitrust violations in a case that was ultimately decided by the U.S. Supreme Court in 1922. This later lawsuit is discussed in the third chapter of this book.

Judge Landis was spared the difficulty of choosing between his pro-antitrust and pro-baseball sentiments in the 1915 trial. (He had played baseball and managed a team as a young man, but declined an offer to play professionally.) Nevertheless, his inclinations were clear in his order of dismissal of the 1915 lawsuit, where he stated that

> "There were two sides to that litigation, what was known and called in the argument here and also throughout the great domain of fandom, Organized Baseball and the outlaws....
>
> And so the question I had to decide, in addition to the legal question submitted, was whether or not I would enter an order that would be vitally injurious if not destructive of Organized Baseball."

With those sentiments, it is clear that "Organized Baseball" chose the right man to be its first Commissioner.

Major League Baseball Is A Uniquely Independent Anti-Competitive Cartel

When it comes to professional sports, Major League Baseball is a law unto itself. Vatican City is an independent nation-state located within Rome, Italy, and operating through its churches and affiliated religious orders in many nations of the world. Major League Baseball is an unincorporated association of National League and American League professional baseball franchises, operating in the United States and Canada. Its member "clubs" also operate training camps and facilities in the Dominican Republic.

Vatican City is unique among nation-states. MLB is a unique entity that is less accountable to its host cities and nations than are the other leagues of professional sports teams. Four characteristics of MLB provide this unique independence.

First, MLB is the only organization of sports teams that has a broad exemption from the antitrust laws of the United States of America. These are the laws that restrict anti-competitive activity in commercial marketplaces.

Second, the unincorporated nature of MLB frees it from supervision under the corporation laws of any state. It is not subject to normal corporate regulations on its governance, operations or disclosures.

Third, from 1999 through 2005, MLB had no governing Constitution that replaced the 1876 National League Constitution and the 1926 American League Constitution. The MLB Constitution established in June 2005 expired at the end of 2012. Since then, MLB has operated without an official Constitution.

You might think that the lack of a formal Constitution would be a hindrance to the operations of MLB. When you are an entity that is beyond the reach of most antitrust laws, however, the absence of a basic governing document, like the absence of a state corporate charter, can be an advantage.

Fourth, the owners of the MLB clubs are all private entities. Since Columbia Broadcasting System (CBS) sold the New York Yankees to George Steinbrenner in 1972, no MLB team has been (or is allowed to be) owned by a public company. As a result, neither MLB itself, nor any MLB franchise, is required to disclose to the public the details of its finances or operations. The leagues' privately owned franchises are often organized as

Limited Liability Companies ("LLCs"), which are less subject to state regulation or scrutiny than regular corporations. This individual club structure fits perfectly within an organization of clubs that is exempt from federal and state antitrust laws.

MLB's antitrust exemption depends on the political acquiescence of a majority of the members of the U.S. Congress. They could vote to eliminate it or limit it at any time.

When local elected officials fear that their city will be unable to get or to keep a major league (or MLB-affiliated minor league) franchise, their Representatives and Senators hear from those local officials. When local elected officials feel pressure from MLB club owners to spend taxpayer money on stadiums for teams owned by millionaires or billionaires, their Representatives and Senators hear from those officials.

In response to pressure by local officials, Representatives and Senators will sometimes propose a bill to eliminate baseball's antitrust exemption. They will hold hearings on their proposals that can place unwanted scrutiny on the operations of "the national pastime".

In 1998, the Congress enacted the "Curt Flood

Act". This law restricted MLB's antitrust exemption by eliminating it in the area of player contracts, specifically the "reserve clause" that had restricted a player's movement to a different team after the expiration of his employment contract.

A lawsuit by an owner of a Major League Baseball club against another club, or against MLB, is rare. MLB owners prefer to resolve internally their disputes, or disputes between an owner and MLB. Peter Angelos, the majority owner of the Baltimore Orioles since 1993, however, is not your typical MLB club owner.

Peter Angelos practiced criminal defense law for twenty years, with labor unions as his frequent clients (like a previous Orioles owner, Edward Bennett Williams). In the 1980s, he shifted his practice to class action litigation. He won more than $100 million in damages for asbestos injuries to shipyard workers. He later won other class action injury lawsuits against Philip Morris and Wyeth. His legal fees from these judgments gave Peter Angelos the money that he used to buy the Baltimore Orioles American League franchise.

PROLOGUE

MLB Club Owners Have Power Under Their Antitrust Exemption to Determine Where Their Competitors Can Operate

In 1990, the San Francisco Giants owners were dissatisfied with their existing stadium and threatened to move to Florida. As an accommodation to them, MLB and the Oakland Athletics club owners agreed that the Giants could relocate to Santa Clara County, California, where San Jose is located. Although they never left San Francisco, the Giants later claimed that Santa Clara was their "exclusive territory". (This designation was written into the 2005 MLB Constitution that expired at the end of 2012, and which has not yet been replaced.)

This "exclusive territory veto" is the subject of a recent lawsuit by the city of San Jose against MLB. The Athletics owners would now like to be able to move their franchise to San Jose. The city of San Jose argues that the designation of San Jose as part of the Giants' exclusive territory was only intended to be effective during the Giants' negotiations with the city of San Francisco to build a new baseball stadium. The Giants argue that the exclusivity was intended to be permanent.

MLB Signed a One-Sided Contract with the Orioles Owner When MLB Owned the Montreal Expos

No designation of Washington, D.C., as the exclusive territory of the Baltimore Orioles, blocked the MLB-owned Montreal Expos' move to Washington. MLB rules only required a majority vote of the owners for the relocation, which they approved in 2004 by a vote of 29-1 (with Angelos's Orioles voting against the move). After the vote, however, Peter Angelos objected to its result and threatened to sue MLB, because he claimed that a new Washington franchise would hurt viewership of, and attendance at, Orioles' games, to a degree that was intolerable. Angelos had previously argued, somewhat inconsistently, that Washington, D.C. would be unable to support an MLB franchise.

In 2005, Peter Angelos negotiated an agreement with MLB that allowed the Montreal Expos franchise to move to Washington, D.C. without the threat of litigation. MLB owned the Expos franchise after buying it from the prior owner (and current Miami Marlins owner), Jeffrey Loria. MLB's earlier plan to contract (eliminate) the Expos franchise was thwarted by a new collective bargaining agreement with the players' union. MLB intended, however, to sell the Expos to a new owner as soon as it could, after moving the Expos to Washington.

Anxious both to get the near-bankrupt Expos off their hands, and to avoid a lawsuit by Peter Angelos, the MLB owners agreed to a contract with Peter Angelos. It was a one-sided contract that heavily favored the Orioles and hampered the Nationals' future owners, whomever they might be. The contract gave the Orioles the rights to a majority ownership of a regional cable sports channel that would telecast both the Orioles' and the Nationals' baseball games. The Orioles would forever own the majority of the shares of the cable channel (without making any capital contribution). The Nationals' ownership share would increase gradually to a maximum of thirty percent.

The Orioles agreed to pay a less-than-market-price annual rights fee to cablecast the Nationals' games from 2005 to 2011. Starting in 2012, for each succeeding five-year period, a new annual rights fee would be paid to the Nationals based on television market factors.

If the Orioles-owned sports channel could not agree with the Nationals on the amount of the post-2011 rights fees, an arbitration panel of three MLB owners would determine the appropriate rights fees.

It would analyze the value of such fees using television market revenue factors already employed for MLB revenue-sharing purposes.

The Orioles and the Nationals 2012 negotiations on the new rights fees were short-lived. When the Orioles' representative presented his offer to the Nationals' representative, the Nationals' man allegedly threw the offer back in his face. The fee dispute then went to the three-person MLB arbitration panel composed of the owners of the New York Mets, Pittsburgh Pirates, and Tampa Bay Rays.

The Washington Nationals argued before the MLB arbitration panel that they should receive $113 million per year from the regional sports channel for telecasts of their baseball games. The Orioles argued that the Nationals should be paid only $34 million per year. In June, 2014 the arbitration panel decided that the Nationals should be paid an amount starting at $53 million per year in 2012 and increasing to $66 million per year in 2016.

Peter Angelos refused to accept this decision as final. Despite the terms of the contract that prohibited any appeal of the decision to a court of law, he sued in the Supreme Court of New York County, where MLB is headquartered, to overturn the MLB arbitration panel decision.

The Nationals Owner, the Judge, and the Lawyers Line Up in Court

The current principal owner of the Washington Nationals, 89-year-old Theodore (Ted) Lerner shuffles through the X-ray and metal detector line with the other court visitors. He takes his seat on a wooden pew. He wears a navy blue suit with a blue dress shirt. His navy blue tie has a pattern of tiny white dots. His black leather shoes have Velcro straps. Lerner pushes his iPhone 6 into his breast pocket. His advisor sitting next to him drops his own phone onto the floor with a bang. Lerner doesn't look or flinch.

Five lawyers for the Nationals/MLB legal team are seated at the table on the left side of the room. They are four men and one woman. One man has gray hair. The others appear to be in their thirties. "Expect anything" says one of the lawyers.

Five lawyers for the MASN/Orioles legal team are seated at the table on the right side of the room. Three are gray-haired men. One is a graying man, and one is a blond woman. They appear to be in their fifties.

Judge Lawrence Marks enters the courtroom. [I will refer to Justice Marks as Judge Marks, as most trial court judges are described.] He vaguely resembles U.S. Supreme Court Justice Stephen Breyer. He speaks softly as he asks the lawyers to not repeat each other's arguments in their presentations. He says that the hearing cannot go over into the afternoon, because of his schedule. It is 9:35 a.m.

1 - THE FIRST INNING – SENATORS, TWINS, EXPOS, NATIONALS, BROWNS AND ORIOLES

"There are only two seasons – Winter and Baseball." – Bill Veeck, Owner of the St. Louis Browns, Cleveland Indians, and Chicago White Sox

At the Hearing

Thomas Hall (Orioles' lawyer):

"What should have happened in the first instance was, when we raised the issues with, 'the Nationals should gave gotten new counsel', they should have seen that they were tainting and poisoning the arbitration…"

The Washington Nationals/Senators (1901-1960)

In 1859, the first semi-professional baseball teams were formed in Washington, D.C. The Potomacs and the Nationals were organized by government workers thirteen years after the first recorded baseball game was played with semi-modern rules in Hoboken, New Jersey by the New York Nine and the New York Knickerbockers.

Other Washington teams followed in the 19th Century, including the Olympics of the National

Association, the Statesmen of the American Association, the Nationals of the Union Association, and the Nationals of the National League from 1885 to 1889, for whom a young Connie Mack (first in games won as a major league manager) played as a catcher. The Senators of the National League followed from 1892 to 1900.

A new Washington team, called the Senators from 1901 to 1904, the Nationals from 1905 to 1955, and called the Senators again from 1956 to 1960, became an original member of the new American League that was formed in 1901. Clark Griffith, a spit-ball throwing pitcher from Missouri, recruited National League players to this new league. He led the Chicago White Sox to the first American League pennant.

After managing the New York Highlanders and the Cincinnati Reds, in 1912 Griffith became the manager of the Washington Nationals. He also became the largest stockholder in the club by buying a 10% ownership stake for $27,000. Griffith mortgaged his six-thousand-acre Montana ranch to finance his purchase.

The Griffith-led Nats jumped from seventh place in 1911 to second place in 1912. That year, AL Most Valuable Player and pitcher Walter

Johnson won 36 games and lost 7, with a 1.14 ERA and eleven shutouts.

Through the 1910s, Griffith acquired the players who would form the basis for the Nats' only World Series championship in 1924: outfielder Sam Rice, first baseman Joe Judge, second baseman/manager "Bucky" Harris, outfielder "Goose" Goslin, and shortstop Roger Peckinpaugh.

On Sunday afternoon, October 10, 1924, in the bottom of the twelfth inning at 5:04 p.m., Earl McNeely bounced the second of two Nationals bad-hop singles in the seventh game of the World Series. It hopped over New York Giants third baseman Freddy Lindstrom's head to win the series for the Nationals. Thirty-six-year-old Walter "The Big Train" Johnson won the game with four innings of scoreless relief pitching, only one day after pitching eight innings and losing game six to the Giants (his second loss of the series).

The Washington Nationals returned to the World Series in 1925, but lost to the Pittsburgh Pirates in seven games. In the 1933 World Series, the Nationals lost to the Giants in five games. Then, the long losing years of Washington baseball began.

Major League Baseball was for many years a

sport of "have" and "have-not" franchises. Sometimes the status of a franchise turned on whether it was located in a big city. Unlike the National Football League, MLB does not split all regular season and playoffs television revenue evenly. The six-month, 162-game baseball season creates regionally popular teams, rather than nationally popular teams.

Some smaller market teams have leveraged their regional popularity, and their management skill. Branch Rickey created the minor league "farm system" when he ran the St. Louis Cardinals franchise. It helped to create consistently successful teams. The New York Yankees have dominated the American League. The Giants and Dodgers (former New York City teams), and the Cardinals have dominated the National League.

The Washington Nationals/Senators' inability to compete with the Yankees led to a humorous aphorism. It twisted an old tribute to George Washington into "Washington – First in War, First in Peace, and Last in the American League".

Decades of baseball futility led Senators fan and author Douglass Wallop to update the medieval German *Faust* legend. In his book *The Year The Yankees Lost the Pennant*, an aging fan, Joe Boyd, trades his soul to the Devil for the body of a young slugger. He is renamed Joe Hardy. Hardy mysteriously appears one day, then leads the Senators to victory in the pennant race over the Yankees. In the 1950s heyday of Broadway musicals, this book was converted into the popular musical *Damn Yankees*.

The Senators lost most of their games after 1933. Worse still, few fans showed up to watch them lose. Clark Griffith owned the team until his death in 1955. He had no external source of wealth, such as a brewery ownership, to cross-promote or to subsidize his baseball business.

In the 1940s, his rentals of Griffith Stadium to the Washington Homestead Grays (seven-time Negro National League champions) brought in valuable revenue. The Senators did not sign their first African-American player until 1954, however, thereby losing an early opportunity to develop an expanded fan base. Griffith tried to compensate for his talent-challenged teams by becoming one of the first owners to sign Cuban baseball players.

None of these strategies helped. When Griffith's nephew, Calvin Griffith Robertson, and his sister Thelma, inherited the ownership of the team in 1955, they soon followed the path of the Boston

Braves, Philadelphia Athletics, Brooklyn Dodgers and New York Giants westward to greener pastures. In 1960, Calvin Griffith Robertson moved the franchise to Minneapolis-St. Paul in Minnesota.

The Expansion Washington Senators (1961-1971)

The National League and the American League knew the potential danger of leaving the nation's capital without a baseball team. Baseball was the most popular American sport. After the Senators moved to Minnesota, rumors grew of a Congressional threat to eliminate baseball's antitrust exemption. A new expansion Washington Senators franchise was granted to the city in 1961, to accompany the new Los Angeles Angels franchise, in an expanded ten-team American League.

The new expansion Senators arrived with few, if any, competitive advantages. They shared a regional baseball fan base with the Baltimore Orioles, who were located only forty-plus miles to the north. They had no minor league farm system. Their owners had no significant wealth with which to subsidize the team. Perhaps, most importantly, the new owners had no business management experience.

Baseball showman Bill Veeck's interest in buying the expansion Senators was rejected by the majority of the league's owners, who resented his maverick reputation and style. Edward Bennett Williams, the future owner of the Washington Redskins and the Baltimore Orioles, made a formal bid for the expansion team. It lost by the vote of one owner – Calvin Griffith.

The expansion Senators struggled for ten years to achieve only one year with a won/loss record above .500. In 1969, the Hall-of-Fame Red Sox outfielder, Ted Williams, managed the Senators to their only winning record at 86-76.

Frank Howard was a four-time All-Star for the Senators, leading the league in home runs with 44 in 1968, and hitting 48 in 1969 and 44 in 1970. Howard was famous for hitting mammoth home runs, including one 500-foot homer that is recognized by a center field upper deck seat painted white, where it landed in R.F.K. Stadium. In 1972, this franchise moved to Dallas-Fort Worth and became the Texas Rangers.

The Wilderness Years End With the Move of the Montreal Expos to Washington, D.C.

After more than one hundred years of baseball,

Washington, D.C. was left without a professional franchise from 1971 until the Montreal Expos franchise moved to the city in 2005. Many excuses were offered for the glaring absence of the "national pastime" in the nation's capital.

Somehow, after one hundred years of baseball, Washington was considered by some club owners to no longer be a "real baseball city". The Baltimore Orioles were said by others to be Washington's baseball team. (This was partly true in that many baseball-starved Washington fans drove to Baltimore to see professional baseball. The Orioles were also owned for a time by the prominent Washington trial lawyer, Edward Bennett Williams.)

Rarely, but occasionally, a subtext for many of these criticisms emerged into public scrutiny, such as the joke that Washington Senators/Minnesota Twins owner Calvin Griffith told at a Lions Club dinner in 1978:

"I'll tell you why we came to Minnesota. It was when we found out you only had 15,000 blacks here. Black people don't go to ballgames, but they'll fill up a rassling ring and put up such a chant it'll scare you to death. We came here because you've got good, hardworking white people here."

After receiving blistering criticism from the Twins' black and Latino players, Calvin Griffith offered the excuse that he had been inebriated when he made his remarks.

The Twins franchise succeeded almost immediately after it moved to Minnesota, using many players who had been developed in the Washington Nationals/Senators/Minnesota Twins farm system, including Hall-of-Fame players Harmon Killebrew and Rod Carew, and Bob Allison, Tony Oliva, and Zoilo Versalles. The Twins won the World Series in 1987 and 1991.

Later, however, the Twins' popularity declined drastically. They played baseball in the Hubert H. Humphrey Metrodome, which was designed primarily as an indoor football stadium. In the new age of chic retro-designed baseball-only stadiums, it was a relic. The Twins posted losing records from 1993 to 2000.

By 2001, the Twins' owner looked for a buyout from MLB that would allow him to extinguish his franchise and to cease its money-losing operations. The equally floundering Montreal Expos baseball franchise provided a convenient counterpart for matching buy-outs proposed by MLB. These buy-outs would have "contracted" the two leagues to fourteen teams each, after the elimination of both franchises.

On November 5, 2001, the Metropolitan Sports Facilities Commission (MSFC), operator of the Metrodome, threatened legal action if the Twins did not fulfill their 2002 lease obligations.

On November 6, 2001, MLB owners meeting in Chicago voted 28-2 to eliminate the Twins and Expos.

On November 7, the MLB Collective Bargaining Agreement (CBA) with the MLB Players Association expired. MLBPA head Donald Fehr had previously announced his expectation that contraction should only be considered as part of the negotiations for the next CBA. On the same day as the owners' vote, Fehr stated that the owners' unilateral decision to shut down two franchises was "the worst manner in which to begin the process of negotiating a new collective bargaining agreement." The loss of two franchises meant the loss of fifty or more major league jobs for players. On November 7, the Players Association filed a grievance that the owners' contraction plan violated their labor contract.

On November 14, U.S. Senator Paul Wellstone

(D-Minn.) and Representative John Conyers (D-Mich.) introduced legislation to eliminate MLB's federal antitrust exemption.

On November 16, a Minnesota judge granted an injunction request by the MSFC to force the Twins to play their 2002 home schedule in the Metrodome.

On December 4, an arbitrator began hearing testimony on the Players Association grievance to block contraction.

On December 6, the U.S. House of Representatives Judiciary Committee held hearings on MLB's antitrust exemption.

On December 20, the owners of the Boston Red Sox voted to sell their American League franchise to the owner of the Miami Marlins, John Henry.

On January 8, 2002, it was revealed that in 1995 a company owned by the Twins' owner, Carl Pohlad loaned $3 million to the MLB Commissioner and Milwaukee Brewers owner Bud Selig and his franchise.

On January 12, The Washington Post reported

that the Expos could be moved to Washington, D.C. for 2003.

After John Henry agreed to make an extra $30 million contribution to charities, the Massachusetts Attorney General withdrew his objection that the charitable trust owner of the Red Sox had not sold the team to the highest bidder, as required by state law.

On January 16, MLB owners officially approved the sale of the Red Sox to John Henry, who agreed to sell the Miami Marlins to the Expos' owner, Jeffrey Loria, for $158.5 million. MLB agreed to buy the Montreal Expos from Loria for $120 million.

On January 17, Commissioner Selig announced that Washington, D.C. was a prime candidate for relocation of the Montreal Expos franchise.

On February 1, MLB owners approved the sale of the Marlins to Loria. The $38.5 million difference between Loria's sale price for the Expos and his purchase price for the Marlins was loaned to him by MLB. The reported terms of the loan were that, if the Marlins did not get a new ballpark within five years, Loria would have to pay back only $23.5 million, and he would not have to pay interest on the loan. If, however, the team got a new ballpark,

MLB would get 20 percent of the team's operating profit during its first five years in the new stadium.

On February 4, the Minnesota Supreme Court refused to consider MLB's appeal of the state court injunction that forced the Twins to perform their 2002 Metrodome lease obligations.

The Twins soon became successful again, winning the American League Central Division in '02, '03, '04, '06, '09 and 2010. In 2010, a new stadium for the Twins, Target Field, opened in downtown Minneapolis.

By 2004, Washington, D.C. had become the overwhelming favorite for the relocation of the Montreal Expos. Between 1972 and 2004, the Washington metropolitan area became one of the ten most populous metropolises in the nation, and perhaps the most affluent. Many baseball hungry Congressmen were prepared to hold more antitrust exemption hearings, if MLB owners blocked the move of the Expos to Washington.

Perhaps most importantly, the city had an aging, but available and serviceable, 50,000-seat baseball stadium. Robert F. Kennedy Stadium had hosted the expansion Senators from 1962 to 1971. Extended negotiations to build a new stadium were not an explicit requirement of the MLB relocation decision. The District of Columbia Council (similar to a state legislature), however, agreed to build a $440 million baseball-only stadium for the new team.

On December 3, 2004, the MLB owners voted 29-1 to approve the relocation of the Montreal Expos to Washington, D.C. Orioles owner Peter Angelos was the one opposing vote. He threatened to sue MLB to stop the relocation.

MLB made a written agreement with Peter Angelos in 2005. In return for his agreement to not sue MLB over the Expos' relocation to Washington, D.C., MLB gave Angelos the rights to broadcast the new Washington team's games on a regional cable sports network, Mid-Atlantic Sports Network (MASN), of which he would be the majority owner.

The new National League Washington Nationals arrived in Washington, D.C. at R.F.K. Stadium for their first home game before a crowd of 45,596 on April 14, 2005. The long thirty-four year wait for the return of major league baseball had ended.

Among the many ironies of the story of the Expos' relocation were: 1) it was the first MLB franchise relocation since the move in 1972 of the expansion Washington Senators to become the Texas Rangers, 2) a Minnesota stadium authority (with some help from the MLB Players Association and Congress) had stopped the MLB plan to eliminate the Expos by obtaining a court injunction requiring the Minnesota Twins (the former Washington Nationals/Senators) to play the 2002 season in Minneapolis-St. Paul, and 3) the new Washington Nationals had moved from Montreal, Canada, the birthplace of the man who had moved the Washington Nationals/Senators to Minnesota, Calvin Griffith Robertson.

The St. Louis Browns/Baltimore Orioles

In the 19th Century, the Baltimore Orioles was the name of a franchise in the American Association (1882-1892) and in the National League (1892-1899). The latter team included "Wee Willie" Keeler who was legendary for his "hit 'em where they ain't" philosophy of baseball. In the "dead ball" era, the Orioles also perfected a technique of hitting the ball in a high bounce off the ground or home plate to allow the batter to reach first safely (the "Baltimore Chop").

Future Hall of Fame manager John McGraw recruited former National League Orioles players for the new American League Orioles in 1901, after the defunct National League Orioles were raided for talent by their Brooklyn Dodgers co-owners. The new American League Orioles played in Baltimore from 1901 to 1903. They moved to New York to become the New York Highlanders, who were later renamed the New York Yankees. By 1902, John McGraw had already taken many of the Orioles' top players (and the black and orange team colors) to the New York Giants.

The Western League Milwaukee Brewers joined the new American League in 1901, but moved to St. Louis after that season to become the St. Louis Browns. The team was popular, but was mostly unsuccessful on the field. In 1916, the team acquired a new owner, Philip Ball, who changed the course of baseball history (for the worst for the Browns) when he fired Browns general manager Branch Rickey in 1919.

Rickey (known as "The Mahatma" for his baseball wisdom and ethical rectitude) became the general manager of the cross-town National League franchise, the Cardinals. In 1923, Ball allowed the Cardinals to become co-tenants with the Browns in the Sportsman's Park stadium. Rickey reinvested the proceeds from the sale of the Cardinals' old ballpark into his new innovation, a minor league "farm" system. He later racially re-integrated baseball by signing Jackie Robinson for the Brooklyn Dodgers in 1947. As the Pittsburgh general manager in 1953, he required that all Pirates players wear batting helmets, another baseball innovation.

From 1927 to 1943 the Browns had only two winning seasons, while their co-tenants, the Cardinals, flourished. On the eve of the Japanese attack on Pearl Harbor, the American League was prepared to vote to approve the move of the Browns to Los Angeles. After the attack, those plans were shelved.

The Browns won their only American League pennant in 1944. All the World Series games were played in Sportsman's Park, where the Browns lost to the Cardinals in six games. More years of futility followed, interrupted only after 1951 by the antics of new owner Bill Veeck. He entertained fans, but infuriated the AL President, by sending 3-foot 7-inch Eddie Gaedel to the plate as a batter. Gaedel walked on four pitches in his only at-bat.

Veeck's attempts to drive the declining Cardinals out of town ended when the Cardinals were purchased by hometown beer baron August Busch. Conceding defeat, Veeck sold Sportsman's Park to the Cardinals. Veeck's attempts to move the

Browns to Milwaukee or Baltimore were blocked by NL owners who resented his previous exploits. The Browns declined to the point that they had to ration batting practice and game baseballs.

In 1954, Veeck was forced out of ownership of the Browns by the other NL owners. The new Browns owners, led by brewery owner Jerold Hoffberger, received quick approval to move the team to Baltimore for the 1954 season. The last Browns owners to profit from their St. Louis legacy were the public shareholders who had bought shares in 1936 to shore up the club's finances. They were bought out by the Orioles owner, Edward Bennett Williams, in 1979.

Beginning with the hiring in 1954 of Paul Richards as manager and general manager, the Orioles developed a reputation for methodical instruction of their players in baseball fundamentals. In 1958, Lee McPhail succeeded Richards as general manager, and improved the Orioles scouting system.

Beginning in 1960, the Orioles steadily improved their performances. In 1964, third baseman Brooks Robinson won the AL Most Valuable Player award. In 1965, the Orioles traded pitcher Milt Pappas to the Cincinnati Reds for 1956

NL Rookie-of-the-Year and 1960 NL Most Valuable Player Frank Robinson. The team won the World Series in 1966, 1970 and 1983.

The Orioles enjoyed eighteen consecutive winning seasons from 1968 to 1985. In 1971, the team had four 20-game winners (Mike Cuellar, Jim Palmer, Pat Dobson, and Dave McNally). John "Boog" Powell won the AL Most Valuable Player Award in 1970. Cal Ripkin, Jr. was AL MVP twice, in 1983 and 1991. In 1995, shortstop Cal Ripkin, Jr. broke Yankee first baseman Lou Gehrig's streak of 2130 consecutive games played. He extended the streak in 1998 to 2,632 games.

In 1992, a new stadium, Orioles Park at Camden Yards, opened in the revitalized Inner Harbor area of downtown Baltimore. The design of the ballpark ushered in a period of "retro" architecture designs in baseball stadiums. These stadiums mixed early 20th century features, like outfield walls of varying distances and features, with modern conveniences. They made 1960s-era shared baseball/football circular stadiums obsolete. Nevertheless, the Orioles suffered fourteen straight losing seasons from 1998 to 2011.

The Washington Nationals Managers Who Came from the Baltimore Orioles

In 1966, Frank Robinson won the American League Most Valuable Player Award (the only player to win the award in both leagues) and became only the tenth MLB player to win the baseball "Triple Crown" for the highest batting average, most home runs, and most runs-batted-in in one season.

The Orioles defeated the Los Angeles Dodgers in four games in the 1966 World Series. They won three consecutive AL pennants from 1969 to 1971, winning the 1970 World Series over the Cincinnati Reds. Frank Robinson was inducted into the MLB Hall of Fame in 1982. Bronze statues of Robinson are located at both Baltimore's Orioles Park and Cincinnati's Great American Ball Park.

Robinson became MLB's first African-American manager with the Cleveland Indians in 1975, and the National League's first African-American manager with the San Francisco Giants in 1981. Robinson was an MLB executive in 2002, when he accepted MLB's request for him to manage the Montreal Expos. He continued to manage the franchise through its transition into the Washington Nationals until 2006.

From 1965 to 1972, Davey Johnson played second base for the Orioles. He later managed the New York Mets to their second World Series victory in 1986 (over the Boston Red Sox). Johnson won AL Manager of the Year honors in 1997 for the Orioles. In the middle of the 2011 season, Johnson became the manager of the Washington Nationals when their previous manager, Jim Riggleman, resigned unexpectedly in the middle of the season.

Johnson led the team to an 80-81 record in 2011. In 2012, the Nationals won their first NL East Division championship, with a major league leading total of 98 wins. Davey Johnson won NL Manager of the Year honors in 2012.

After falling back to an 86-76 record in 2013, Johnson was replaced in 2014 by Matt Williams. Williams won Manager of the Year honors in 2014, leading the team to a 96-66 record and its second NL East pennant. After falling back to an 83-79 record in 2015, Williams was fired and replaced by John "Dusty" Baker on November 3, 2015.

Baker played in the National League and the American League for nineteen years, primarily for the Atlanta Braves, and Los Angeles Dodgers, with whom he won a World Championship in 1981. Beginning in 1993, Baker managed the San Francisco Giants, the Chicago Cubs and the Cincinnati Reds. He was named National League Manager of the Year in 1993, 1997, and 2000.

2 - THE SECOND INNING – SOLDIERS, CLERKS, STEELMAKERS, DEALMAKERS AND LITIGATORS

"A hot dog at the ballpark is better than steak at the Ritz." – Humphrey Bogart, American actor

At the Hearing

Mr. Neuwirth (Nationals' lawyer):

"It's purely speculative to assert that the fact that these relationships existed at the time somehow means that there was an undue influence on the process, and we're going to see just the opposite occurred."

Judge Marks:

"Look, I can't believe the rule is that extreme. Obviously this wasn't the case here, but what if Proskauer was personally representing each of the arbitrators on this Committee, each of the three, while the arbitration was pending? You're saying that that wouldn't be enough?....

You know something, if that's the law, with all due respect, that doesn't make any sense. It really doesn't...."

Mr. Neuwirth:

"Well, at the very least, we don't have something that extreme here, as I think your Honor recognized."

Judge Marks:

"I agree with that."

The Dealmaker

In 1921, Theodore "Ted" Lerner's father, Mayer, emigrated from Palestine to the U.S., where he met his wife-to-be, Ethel, who had emigrated from Lithuania. In Washington, D.C., in 1925, their first child, Ted, was born into their household at Georgia Avenue and Otis Street.

In a 2007 interview, Lerner recalled

"Rye bread was nine cents. I remember chickens being plucked and koshered on Georgia Avenue. Posin's was our delicatessen. We got around by walking or taking streetcars."

Georgia Avenue, where the Lerners lived, had an important, although mostly forgotten, history during the Civil War. At that time, it was known as the 7th Street Turnpike. It was a wooden plank road extending from the border of the City of Washington (where "Boundary Field" would later be built, expanded and renamed Griffith Stadium) to the District of Columbia/Maryland line.

During the Civil War, Abraham Lincoln often rode up the 7th Street Turnpike to the Soldier's Home for retired military. There, a large cottage on the third highest hill in the District served as his summer White House. On July 11, 1865, battle-hardened soldiers of the Union Army VI and XIX Corps were rushed by steamboats from the Siege of Richmond to resist a surprise invasion of Washington, D.C.

Between ten and twenty thousand soldiers of Confederate Lieutenant General Jubal Early's Second Corps of the Army of Northern Virginia escaped the Richmond siege. They marched through the Shenandoah Valley of Virginia and through western Maryland to Washington.

Lincoln greeted the Union soldiers as they disembarked from their steamboats. He joked with them that "You can't be late if you want to get Early."

Early's troops were delayed by a Union Army resistance at the Monocacy River in Maryland. It was led by Major General Lew Wallace. Wallace was blamed by Ulysses S. Grant for the Union Army's stalemated invasion of Mississippi at the earlier Battle of Shiloh. He was also the post-war author of the popular novel *Ben-Hur*.

At the three-day Battle of Fort Stevens on July 11, 12 and 13, 1865, at the 7th Street Turnpike and Military Road, President Lincoln became the only U.S. President (other than James Madison at the War of 1812 Battle of Bladensburg) to come under enemy fire in wartime. While visiting the fort on either July 12 or 13, Lincoln was reported to have stood on a parapet in his stove-pipe hat. He drew the fire of a sharpshooter, who wounded an Army surgeon standing behind him. Some historians estimate that as many as eight hundred soldiers from both sides died in this battle that turned back the Confederacy's last invasion of the North.

As a child, Lerner sold copies of the *Saturday Evening Post* magazine door-to-door to earn enough money to pay 25 cents for a bleacher seat to watch the Senators play in Griffith Stadium. "I was an usher at the all-star game when Dizzy Dean was hit on the foot by a line drive," he recalled. "He was never the same after that."

Lerner graduated from Roosevelt High School in 1944, where his gym teacher was Arnold "Red" Auerbach, the future coach of the National Basketball Association Boston Celtics. Bowie Kuhn, the future MLB commissioner, was a friend and classmate.

At Roosevelt High School, Lerner learned to type. He became the editor of the *Rough Rider*, the school newspaper. After graduating and being drafted into the Army, he boarded a train of soldiers headed to Europe, where many of those soldiers would fight, be wounded and die in the Battle of the Bulge.

"An officer boarded the train, called my name, and took me off," he recalled. "They needed a typist at the base." Lerner served the remainder of the war in that capacity.

After the war ended, with financial support from the "G. I. Bill", Lerner enrolled at George Washington University, where he received an Associate's degree and a law degree. Before he started classes, however, his father died on Ted's 21st birthday. Ted Lerner became responsible for the care of his mother, and his younger brother and sister.

"I was always interested in real estate," he told an interviewer. "I started selling homes on weekends when I was in law school. I have an instinct for it."

Ted Lerner sold thousands of homes in the suburban Maryland towns of College Park and Wheaton (named after Union Brigadier General Frank Wheaton who commanded a brigade at the Battle of Fort Stevens). To accomplish that

"I just worked. I took off for Jewish holidays and a Redskin game or two. It was nothing to do 18-hour days.... I came home for dinner with the family every night.... I had an office on Georgia Avenue in those days, two blocks away from the apartment. I would eat, go back to the office, and work until 2 am."

As Debra Lerner Cohen remembered her mother's approach to life,

"She was a hands-on mom. Those were pre-nanny days. She drove us to Hebrew school, ballet class, made dinner, kept kosher. We did not stick out.... In my mind we weren't rich. I recall my mom telling me things were too expensive, to not be wasteful, to not take things for granted. We had curfews. We had rules. I would say we were somewhat sheltered."

By the 1960s, Ted Lerner had built strong banking relationships that enabled him to team up with other developers to build shopping malls near the Interstate 495 "Beltway". This highway opened in 1964 and encircled Washington, D.C. and its inner suburbs.

Lerner's first suburban mall, Wheaton Plaza, opened in 1960. Simultaneously, Lerner bought and leased hundreds of acres of farmland at a country crossroads fifteen miles outside of Washington, D.C., called Tysons Corner.

Virginia State Route 267 was built just to the north of Tysons Corner for the new Dulles International Airport that opened in 1962. Parallel toll-road lanes were later added to it to accommodate the booming suburbs of Fairfax County, Virginia. The new Beltway crossed just east of Tysons Corner in 1966. The new Interstate 66 highway was built just south of Tysons Corner in 1982.

These new roads brought new families and shoppers to what had been rural Northern Virginia. Lerner built office buildings and two malls at Tysons Corner. It grew into one of the largest shopping centers in the world. He bought thousands more acres of undeveloped land in the 1980s near Dulles International Airport. He later developed that land into office buildings and retail centers.

Only one of Lerner's projects failed. The Landover Mall in suburban Prince George's County, Maryland opened in 1972, near the Capital Center sports arena. It was built by Abe Pollin, another D.C. developer-turned-sports-franchise-owner, for his NBA basketball team, the Bullets, and his new NHL hockey team, the Capitals.

Landover Mall was bulldozed by Lerner in 2002, after years of failing to find enough retail tenants. The property is still owned by Lerner and his family members. Ed Cohen, one of Lerner's sons-in-law said in an interview that "We will build something there, but we don't know yet what that will be." That approach works well in a business that rewards long term investment horizons, and that reduces income taxes on inherited property.

Lerner weathered the late 1980s real estate downturn by diversifying into private equity buyouts, including the purchase of bankrupt Continental Airlines. Ted Lerner has delegated day-to-day responsibilities to his son, Mark Lerner, and to his brothers-in-law Ed Cohen and Bob Tannenbaum. They keep the family business going through constant communication and shared vacation time with their families on Kent Island, Maryland. They have monthly family meetings to talk about business and family matters.

Ted Lerner offered to buy the Baltimore Orioles in 1979, but their owner, Jerold Hoffberger, sold the team to D.C. lawyer Edward Bennett Williams. The Lerners won the competition to acquire the Nationals franchise from its MLB owners in 2006 for $450 million. The Lerners' wealth, their discretion, and their family cohesiveness appealed to the MLB owners, who prefer to avoid controversy regarding the business of baseball. The Lerners' persistence in goal–setting and long-term investing was essential to rebuild the Expos farm system that had been raided for talent by rival MLB owners.

The Litigator

Four years after Ted Lerner was born in Washington, D.C., Peter Angelos was born on the 4th of July in Pittsburgh to parents who had immigrated from Greece. As a child, he helped serve steelworkers at his parents' tavern in the Highlandtown section of Baltimore.

After graduating from Eastern College of Law, Angelos graduated from the University of Baltimore School of Law, where he was class valedictorian. He was elected to the Baltimore City Council from 1959 to 1963. In 1967, he ran for Mayor of Baltimore, becoming the first candidate to run on a racially integrated ticket. He ran three times unsuccessfully for the Maryland legislature as a Democratic candidate.

Despite his history of public service, Peter Angelos, like Ted Lerner, rarely speaks about himself. He has been married for 49 years to his wife, Georgia, and has two sons, John and Lou, the latter of whom works in the Angelos law office.

In 1961, Peter Angelos opened his law firm practicing criminal defense law. Many of his clients were Baltimore labor unions and their members. In 1982, Angelos became one of the first lawyers to represent class action plaintiffs for asbestos injuries. When one lawsuit was eventually settled in 1992 for more than $1 billion, Angelos's share of the settlement was reportedly worth more than $100 million.

Peter Angelos continues to work at his law offices. He has litigated other successful class action personal injury settlements, judgments and verdicts, such as the State of Maryland's $4.5 billion recovery against tobacco company Philip Morris, and a class action against drugmaker Wyeth for injuries from its diet pill combination fen-phen.

Angelos used his new wealth to lead a group of investors in 1993 to purchase the Baltimore Orioles franchise from the bankruptcy estate of former owner Eli Jacobs for $173 million. The value of the baseball team has more than doubled since its purchase.

The greatest addition to Peter Angelos's wealth, however, has come from his negotiation with Major League Baseball for the terms of his agreement to not litigate the Montreal Expos relocation to Washington, D.C. in 2005. This agreement allowed Angelos to create a new regional cable sports network, Mid-Atlantic Sports Network (MASN) to cablecast both Orioles and Nationals games. The agreement with MLB guarantees at least 70% of the ownership of MASN to the Orioles owner.

In 2010, MASN was estimated to be worth roughly $600 million, while the Orioles were separately estimated to be worth about $360 million. Peter Angelos intended the profits from cablecasting the games of two baseball teams, including the Washington team's games in a larger television market, to help him to compete against the billionaire owners of the Boston Red Sox and New York Yankees.

From 1998 to 2009, the Orioles posted twelve consecutive losing seasons. Since 2010, however, the Orioles have made the playoffs in 2012 and 2014, posting three consecutive winning seasons.

3 - THE THIRD INNING - AN ANTITRUST EXEMPTION CREATES A MAJOR LEAGUE BASEBALL CARTEL

"cartel 1. A group of businesses or nations that collude to limit competition within an industry or market."- from *Wiktionary*

At the Hearing

Judge Marks:

"Well, if they have incorrectly applied the methodology, applied the wrong methodology, would I be able to second-guess that?"

Mr. Neuwirth (Nationals' lawyer):

"If all it says is 'apply the established methodology,' and the arbitrators undertake to apply the established methodology, even if you think they were completely wrong in how they did that, you cannot reverse them. You cannot vacate the award. And the case law, which we will look at, says that…."

The U.S. Supreme Court in 1922 Creates An Antitrust Exemption for Baseball

U.S. antitrust laws prohibit various anti-competitive practices. Exemptions to the laws apply, however, to a variety of businesses and actors. The Clayton Act of 1914 provides that human labor was "not a commodity or article of commerce." Therefore, collective action by employees (like union bargaining) or consumers (like boycotts) is permitted. Professional football, baseball, basketball and hockey teams are allowed by federal statutes to make joint agreements on the broadcasting of their league games.

A competitor to the National and American leagues, the Federal League, folded in 1915. Most of its club owners were compensated by National League and American League owners in some way. For example, the St. Louis Terriers club owner was allowed to buy the St. Louis Browns of the American League. The ballpark now known as Wrigley Field was built in 1914 as Weeghman Park for the Federal League Chicago Whales. The Chicago Cubs relocated there in 1916.

The dissatisfied former owner of the Federal League Baltimore Terrapins, however, sued the National League and the American League for conspiring to monopolize baseball by destroying the Federal League. A trial court found the defendants liable under the Clayton Antitrust Act.

In the 1922 decision of *Federal Baseball Club of Baltimore v. National League of Professional Baseball Clubs*, U.S. Supreme Court Justice Oliver Wendell Holmes wrote a unanimous opinion for the Court, stating that professional baseball was not "interstate commerce", and that it was therefore exempt from federal antitrust laws.

Holmes wrote that, despite the interstate travel required to accomplish it,

> "[T]he giving of exhibitions of baseball ... are purely state affairs.... [T]he transport is a mere incident, not the essential thing. That to which it is incident, the exhibition, although made for money, would not be called trade or commerce in the commonly accepted use of those words. As it is put by defendant, personal effort not related to production is not a subject of commerce. That which in its consummation is not commerce does not become commerce among the states because the transportation that we have mentioned takes place. To repeat the illustrations given by the court below, a firm of lawyers sending out a member to argue a case,

or the Chautauqua lecture bureau sending out lecturers, does not engage in such commerce because a lawyer or lecturer goes to another state.

If we are right, the plaintiff's business is to be described in the same way, and the restrictions by contract that prevented the plaintiff from getting players to break their bargains and the other conduct charged against the defendants were not an interference with commerce among the states."

The Supreme Court Later Admits That Its 1922 Decision Was A Mistake, But Refuses to Correct It

After 1922, the baseball antitrust exemption (unique in its breadth and specific application to one sport) could have been overturned by a later Supreme Court decision, or by an act of Congress. Twice, however, the Supreme Court refused to overturn the exemption.

In the 1953 *Toolson v. New York Yankees, Inc.* decision, the Supreme Court upheld, by a 7-2 vote, the baseball antitrust exemption, and the "reserve clause" requirement of player contracts that since the 1880s had prevented player free agency. Like a "covenant to not compete" in an employment contract, the mandatory reserve clause in every player contract prohibited any player from playing for a new team for one year after his contract expired, without the permission of his previous team. Unlike other employment agreements, however, the player contract could be unilaterally renewed every year by the team employer, making the player a perpetual employee (if he wanted to stay in baseball). The Court interpreted the failure of Congress to overturn its 1922 decision as an implicit approval of baseball's antitrust exemption.

The questionable logic of the *Federal Baseball Club* and *Toolson* decisions was highlighted by the 1955 U.S. Supreme Court decision denying an antitrust exemption to professional boxing matches. Chief Justice Warren wrote for the majority that

> "[T]his Court has never before considered the antitrust status of the boxing business. Yet, were it not for *Federal Baseball* and *Toolson*, we think that it would be too clear for dispute."

In other words, without the dubious Supreme Court antitrust decisions on baseball, boxing should not have wasted its time or money on arguments for a similar exemption.

Justice Frankfurter dissented, writing that

> "[I]t would baffle the subtlest ingenuity to find a single differentiating factor between other sporting exhibitions ... and baseball insofar as the conduct of the sport is relevant to the criteria or considerations by which the Sherman [Antitrust] Law becomes applicable to a 'trade or commerce'."

Justice Minton, also dissented, adding

> "What this Court held in the *Federal Baseball* case to be incident to the exhibition [interstate travel] now becomes more important than the exhibition. This is as fine an example of the tail wagging the dog as can be conjured up."

A 1957 Supreme Court decision denied the NFL an antitrust exemption in *National Football League v. Radovich*. The best justification offered by the majority for maintaining MLB's exemption was described by Justice Clark in that case as

> "[M]ore harm would be done in overruling *Federal Baseball* than in upholding a ruling which, at best, was of dubious validity.... Were we considering the question of baseball for the first time upon a clean slate, we would have no

doubts."

In other words, despite the Justices' belief that baseball should not be exempt from antitrust laws, the unspecified detriments of correcting the Court's earlier mistake (except for mentions of a "flood of litigation", "harassment", and its "retroactive effect") would be worse than the benefits of correcting it.

In the 1972 Supreme Court case of *Flood v. Kuhn*, St. Louis Cardinals all-star center fielder Curt Flood challenged the validity of the baseball reserve clause by refusing a 1969 trade to the Philadelphia Phillies. In a 5-3 decision, the Court upheld the reserve clause on the basis of the same argument that undoing a long-standing wrong decision would be worse than leaving it alone. It added the reasoning that, by acquiescing in the antitrust exemption, Congress had signaled its approval of it.

Curt Flood sat out the 1970 baseball season. He agreed to a trade to the Washington Senators for the 1971 season, where he appeared in only 13 games, before he retired.

The Players Union Slays the Reserve Clause Dragon

The Major League Baseball Players Association was formed in 1953. It made little progress in negotiations with the leagues, however, until 1966, when it hired United Steelworkers of America negotiator Marvin Miller to be its Executive Director.

In 1968, Miller negotiated the first Collective Bargaining Agreement (CBA) with team owners, which raised the minimum player salary from $6,000 to $10,000 per year. The 1970 CBA required labor disputes to be decided by arbitration.

In 1975, an arbitrator ruled that Los Angeles Dodgers pitcher Andy Messersmith and Montreal Expos pitcher Dave McNally became free agents after playing one year for their team without a signed contract. Teams had previously renewed expiring contracts unilaterally without a player signature, thereby binding players to their teams for as long as the team desired. The players' union won the teams' appeal of the decision in federal court.

In 1976, the Major League Baseball Players Association and MLB signed a collective bargaining agreement that allowed players with six years of

MLB experience to become free agents. In 1998, the federal "Curt Flood Act" established antitrust protection for major league baseball players to the same extent as other professional athletes. Minor league baseball players and other MLB operations, however, remain ungoverned by antitrust laws.

Player Drafts, Revenue Sharing, the Luxury Tax, and Post-Season Playoffs Have Made More MLB Clubs Competitive

In 1965, MLB started its first draft of amateur college players, thereby reducing the power of teams with deep farm systems like the Yankees. Since the 1940s, MLB teams have also participated in drafts of certain players who remain on minor league teams beyond a specified number of years. These drafts place the teams with the worst previous year records in the best drafting positions. They reduce the power of the teams with the best records, or richest owners, to buy the best young players, or to stockpile good players in their farm systems.

Since 2006, MLB teams have also agreed to revenue-sharing of 31% of net local revenues, and national television contracts. In 2016, only the teams in the 15 smallest media markets are scheduled to receive full revenue sharing. Revenue-sharing can be used to build quality team rosters, or it can be used to build a team owner's wealth.

In 2005, the Florida Marlins payroll was only $14,998,500. That same year, the Marlins reportedly received $31 million from revenue-sharing, which the MLB collective bargaining agreement states must be used for "baseball-related activities". Kansas City Royals revenue-sharing income doubled from 2002 to 2007, but the Royals payroll only rose by 6%. The estimated value of the franchise, however, rose from $96 million to $282 million.

Since 1994, a so-called Luxury Tax has applied to team payrolls above a certain level (after the players' union rejected a National Football League type of salary cap). Since 2002, money from this "Competitive Balance Tax" goes mostly to fund player benefits, the "Industry Growth Fund" for training camps and baseball development activities, and to baseball development in countries without high school programs. Although the Luxury Tax does not directly benefit lower payroll clubs, it does penalize high payroll clubs, like the New York Yankees and Los Angeles Dodgers.

Until 1969, the World Series was the only post-season competition in Major League Baseball. The first-place finishers in the American and National Leagues played each other for the World Series championship, and that was it.

Since 1969, three levels of intra-league playoffs have been added: 1) a one game playoff between the fifth-best and fourth-best "wild card" teams, 2) two best-of-five playoff series, one between the surviving wild card teams and the two teams with the best regular season records in three divisions, and one between the second-best and third-best division champions, and 3) one best-of-seven series between the survivors of the five-game series playoffs.

The expanded playoffs format allows ten of the thirty MLB teams to play into the "post-season". This is the lowest percentage of playoff teams among the major professional U.S. team sports. It provides late-season hope, however, to smaller market teams that, before 1969, had far fewer chances to win a championship.

The effects of the player drafts, revenue sharing, the Luxury Tax, and the post-season playoffs have been to increase the capabilities of smaller market teams to compete against larger market teams like the New York, Los Angeles and Chicago teams. Does the antitrust exemption decrease professional baseball competition in any significant ways that are not compensated for by these MLB procedures? The answers to that question depend, as many antitrust questions depend, on the definition of the relevant competitive market.

How Has the Antitrust Exemption Hurt Baseball Competition?

If the relevant market is defined as the market for more talented MLB baseball players, the MLB procedures that increase competition within the leagues compensate moderately for the anti-competitive effects of large market regional television and stadium revenues. Unlike the National Football League, a club's regional television revenues can be greater than its share of national television revenues. The larger populations of big cities also create larger stadium attendance revenues for their local teams over a 162-game season, regardless of the team quality.

MLB franchise owners have argued that application of antitrust laws to professional baseball would upset its delicate competitive balance, because money-losing teams would move to the biggest cities to participate in the larger available revenues. They argue that the current systems promote greater competition than would exist in a total free market for teams, because strict antitrust law enforcement would prohibit the competitive balancing procedures of the drafts, revenue sharing and the luxury tax.

Without the benefit of a national television contract, such as the NFL and NBA contracts, which provide equal and substantial contract revenue shares to all teams, MLB teams are in a less advantageous competitive context. Nevertheless, the protection of all competitors in an existing market against competition from market outsiders is not a normal objective of antitrust laws.

If the relevant antitrust market is defined not as the current MLB lineup of teams, it could be defined as the potential free market of existing and new competitors for professional baseball talent. This potential market might even be one answer to the nagging existential dilemma of baseball, which is its declining attractiveness to talented young athletes and to young spectators.

In the aftermath of the *Federal League* Supreme Court decision in 1922, no other professional baseball league has been successfully organized to compete with the National and American Leagues. In the 1930s, the Mexican League attracted some MLB players, but "black-balling" of these players by

MLB owners soon led to that league's demise. The seven leagues, beginning in 1920, which are referred to as the Negro Leagues, quickly lost their talent to the National League and the American League after the former's integration by Jackie Robinson in 1947.

The National Football League faced the competing All-American Football Conference from 1945 to 1949, before absorbing its three best teams, the Cleveland Browns, the San Francisco Forty-Niners and the Baltimore Colts. From 1960 to 1966, the NFL competed against the American Football League, before agreeing to a merger in 1966 that led to a complete takeover of the AFL by the NFL in 1970.

Major League Baseball, unlike the NFL, did not absorb any teams from the competing Mexican or Negro Leagues. After the 1953 *Toolson* Supreme Court decision, no would-be professional baseball league competitors have emerged. This could be attributed to historical anti-competitive MLB practices to discourage such outside competition.

In addition, current MLB practices control internal competition, including required league approval for league expansion to more teams, and for the relocation of teams, including relocation into the geographic "territory" of an existing team.

The antitrust protection against external and internal competition that MLB enjoys, however, might have caused a stagnation of its competitive skills regarding fan satisfaction, rules changes, and the training and encouragement of young baseball players. The average age of an MLB baseball fan is 53 years old (about the same as for opera fans), compared to 47 years for NFL fans, and 37 years for National Basketball Association fans.

Antitrust protection and anti-competitive MLB practices might provide larger profits to current owners than they would receive without such protection and practices. Some current players might receive larger salaries if more than two leagues were available to bid for their services. Current minor league players, coaches, managers and executives, whose chances for higher salaries are limited by the restrictions on the size of major league payrolls, would certainly benefit from the competition provided by a new major league, and from a collective bargaining agreement, like the one that benefits players in the two major leagues.

City of San Jose v. MLB Lawsuit Over the Oakland A's Franchise Relocation – The End of the Antitrust Free Ride for MLB?

On June 28, 2013, the City of San Jose, California, filed a lawsuit in the United States District Court for the Northern District of California against Major League Baseball. *City of San Jose v. Office of the Commissioner of Baseball* alleged various acts by MLB injuring the city, including torts (personal injuries), such as tortious interference with contract (the city's ballpark land purchase option agreement with the Oakland Athletics), California unfair competition and antitrust statute violations, and Federal antitrust violations. These injuries allegedly were caused by a "blatant conspiracy by Major League Baseball ("MLB") to prevent the Athletics Baseball Club from moving to San Jose."

The lawsuit alleged a "dark side" to this "uniquely American sport" in that

"MLB has unlawfully conspired to control the location and relocation of major league men's professional baseball clubs under the guise of an 'antitrust exemption' applied to the business of baseball."

The suit alleged that MLB internal rules require three-quarters of the teams in a league to approve the relocation of a team, which is allowed only in "the most dire of circumstances where a local community has, over a sustained period, demonstrated that it cannot or will not support a franchise."

In this case, San Jose alleged that it was unreasonably restricted by MLB from competing with the City of Oakland for the Athletics Baseball Club. San Jose cited Article VI, Section 2(b)(3) of the 2005 MLB Constitution as granting each club "absolute veto power over the relocation of a competitive team within its 'operating territory'."

This provision only required a three-quarters vote of all MLB clubs for relocation. Nevertheless, Article VIII, Section 8 stated that "The Major League Clubs shall have assigned operating territories within which they have the right and obligation to play baseball games as the home Club."

San Jose alleged that these MLB internal business rules create a monopoly in violation of Section 2 of the Sherman Act. In addition the city alleged that MLB and its clubs, as an "illegal cartel", created exclusive television and radio broadcast rights within designated operating territories.

San Jose cited a 1998 complaint against MLB by the New York Yankees in a New York federal trial court. The Yankees complained that MLB operated as a cartel in which "Clubs have agreed not to compete with each other." The subject of this 1998 lawsuit was the Yankees' attempt to make a licensing agreement with the sportswear company Adidas, without MLB's permission. The Yankees case was settled on a confidential basis, however, without any hearing on its merits.

Also cited by San Jose is the 2010 U.S. Supreme Court opinion in *American Needle, Inc. v. National Football League*. In this decision, the Supreme Court reaffirmed lower court decisions that sports leagues are subject to the antitrust laws. It reaffirmed its 1984 decision, in *NCAA v. Board of Regents*, that "the hallmark of an unreasonable restraint is one that raises price, lowers output, or renders output unresponsive to consumer preference."

San Jose alleged that one example of the effect of MLB's anticompetitive restrictions is that, absent exclusive territorial arrangements, teams would arrange for their own games to be available in other teams' broadcast markets. The MLB restrictions, however, force fans to pay for more games than they want to pay for, and for games that they don't want to watch.

The MLB argument that its restrictions are necessary to maintain competitive balance were countered with a City of San Jose argument that revenue sharing is already a less restrictive alternative to territorial rights. The city argued that it could be expanded to make up for team revenue disparities that might result from greater competition.

The City of San Jose lawsuit against MLB has its origins in a 1990 threat by the owners of the San Francisco Giants to move their franchise. Both Tampa, Florida and San Jose, California were considered for relocation. The Athletics owner, Walter Haas, gave his verbal consent to the relocation of the Giants to the County of Santa Clara, which includes the City of San Jose. This generous "good deed" by Haas, who was a Levi Strauss clothing company heir, is reminiscent of Senators owner Clark Griffith's uncompensated consent to the American League St. Louis Browns relocation to Baltimore in 1954.

In 1990, the Giants owner, Bob Lurie, was very dissatisfied with the Giants' city-owned ballpark, Candlestick Park. He pursued a new city-built park in San Jose. According to San Jose's lawsuit, however, Haas "never granted the Giants an exclusive right to Santa Clara County [forever], only his consent to pursue relocation of the Club to Santa Clara County in 1990." After the San Jose voters rejected plans to build a new ballpark for the Giants, however, the Athletics club never acted to formally re-establish its exclusive rights in Santa Clara County.

The Changing MLB Rules on Franchise Exclusive Territory Rights

MLB rules on club exclusive territory rights have changed over time. In 1876, the National League Constitution gave each team control over a five-mile radius around its home city.

By 1960, different league rules applied to home territory rights. National League rules defined a home territory as expanding to a ten-mile radius beyond a club's home city limits. American League rules defined a home territory as a 100-mile radius around a club's home ballpark. Territory rights were only applied within each league, until Major League Baseball was formed as an unincorporated association in 2000.

The consent of the National League San

Francisco Giants, for example, was not required for the American League Kansas City Athletics to move to Oakland, California in 1966, although Oakland is less than ten miles from San Francisco. The irony (or hypocrisy) of exclusive geographic territory rights is illustrated by the fact that if the Oakland Athletics club moved to San Jose, it would be thirty-two miles farther from the Giants' current ballpark than the current Athletics location in Oakland.

Article VIII, Section 8 of the 2005 Major League Constitution, in effect until the end of 2012, defined the "Operating Territories" of each club with geographic descriptions, such as city and county, with specific provisos if a territory is shared with another franchise, such as the Yankees-Mets, Dodgers-Angels, and Cubs-White Sox territories. The 2005 MLB Constitution defined the Giants territory by adding a proviso that "with respect to all Major League Clubs, Santa Clara County in California shall also be included."

The 2005 Constitution, making Santa Clara County part of the Giants' territory, and requiring a three-quarters vote of the clubs to approve a franchise relocation, is not currently in effect. It is very likely, however, that these same rules would be applied in an unwritten form to any proposed relocation of the Athletics franchise.

The current Major League Rules, Attachment 52, makes Santa Clara County part of the Giants' territory, and current Rule 1(c)(2) still refers to "a Major League Club [transferring] its location to another home territory after approval is obtained under the Major League Constitution", even though the only Major League Constitution ever created is no longer in effect.

The Effect of MLB Relocation Rules on the Orioles-Nationals-MLB Rights Fees Arbitration

Under Article VI, Section 1, of the expired MLB Constitution, all MLB clubs agreed that any disputes among them shall be decided by the MLB Commissioner as the sole dispute arbitrator. Section 2 provides that

> "[T]he Clubs ... agree to be finally and unappealably bound by actions of the Commissioner ... and ... waive such right of recourse to the courts as would otherwise have existed in their favor."

Section 2 also provides, however, that

"In the event of any legal action other than as prescribed by Section 1 ... the Commissioner may direct that the costs [to MLB of that action] ... be reimbursed to the Office of the Commissioner ... by such non-complying Club."

This reimbursement of costs "penalty" could be interpreted as allowing a "recourse to the courts" of an "action of the Commissioner", if MLB is reimbursed for any costs of responding to such a recourse.

Washington, D.C., and its adjacent suburban counties were never designated as part of the Baltimore Orioles' exclusive territory. Consequently, the rules on appealing to the courts the MLB Commissioner's resolution of inter-team disputes might have been invoked to prevent any appeal by Peter Angelos, the Orioles owner, of the 2004 vote of his fellow owners (29-1) to relocate the Montreal Expos to Washington.

The other MLB owners decided instead to placate Peter Angelos. They gave him a contract assigning to him the permanent right to control the regional cable telecasts of Nationals' games. In doing so, the owners surrendered MLB's option to invoke their Constitution's ambivalent ban on "recourse to the courts". In return, Peter Angelos agreed to not litigate over the Expos' relocation to Washington, D.C. The current lawsuit over the cablecast rights fees is, arguably, not covered by Angelos's promise not to sue over the Expos' relocation. In any event, the Article VI ban on "recourse to the courts" applied to "actions of the Commissioner", rather than to an arbitration panel's award, and it expired with the MLB Constitution in 2012.

[Reader Alerts – See page 125 for the text of the 2005 Television Contract stating that the parties would not appeal an MLB arbitration panel award to a court except on "grounds of corruption, fraud or miscalculation of figures."

See page 131-132 for the text of Commissioner Selig's 2014 letter to the Orioles and Nationals chastising them for litigating the 2014 MLB arbitration, and threatening to sanction them for litigating.]

The Federal Ninth Circuit Court of Appeals Decision Affirms the Dismissal of the *City of San Jose* Lawsuit

In October 2013, a trial judge in the federal District Court for the Northern District of

California granted MLB's motion to dismiss the federal and state antitrust claims, and the state unfair competition claim, in the *City of San Jose* lawsuit. Judge Whyte relied on the line of U.S. Supreme Court baseball antitrust exemption decisions reaching back to *Federal Baseball Club* in 1922. He also interpreted the failure by Congress to enact legislation to overturn the exemption as a tacit approval of it.

In January 2015, the U.S. Court of Appeals for the Ninth Circuit reviewed San Jose's appeal of the dismissal. San Jose argued on appeal that the *Flood v. Kuhn* decision should be limited to an antitrust exemption for the specific issue in that case of the "reserve clause". The appeals court rejected this argument, because, in its 1974 decision of *Portland Baseball Club, Inc. v. Kuhn*, it had already applied a broader interpretation of the antitrust exemption. It had used the exemption to dismiss an argument that MLB acted as a monopoly in approving a new major league team in the previously exclusive territory of a minor league team.

The Ninth Circuit dismissed the argument that MLB franchise relocation decisions were insufficiently related to "baseball's unique characteristics and needs" (*Flood*) to warrant exemption from antitrust laws. "The designation of franchises to particular geographic territories is the league's basic organizing principle", stated Judge Kozinski, citing a 1982 Seventh Circuit decision rejecting an antitrust challenge to franchise relocation restrictions in *Professional Baseball School and Clubs, Inc. v. Kuhn.*

Finally, the Ninth Circuit noted that Congress enacted the 1998 "Curt Flood Act". The Act eliminated the baseball antitrust exemption regarding the player reserve clause, but it expressly addressed the exemption for franchise relocation matters, by stating that

> "This section does not create, permit or imply a cause of action by which to challenge under the antitrust laws, or otherwise apply the antitrust laws to ... franchise []location or relocation."

San Jose's state law antitrust and unfair competition claims could not survive the dismissal of its federal antitrust claims, because they alleged the same violations. Federal law superseded them, because "national uniformity is required in any regulation of baseball." The Ninth Circuit concluded that

> "Only Congress and the Supreme Court are empowered to question *Flood's* continued

vitality, and with it, the fate of baseball's singular and historic exemption from the antitrust laws."

On October 5, 2015, the U.S. Supreme Court refused to review the Ninth Circuit's approval of the trial court's dismissal of San Jose's antitrust claims against MLB.

An Active Lawsuit Challenges Minor League Player Movement Restrictions, and Another Lawsuit Claims Minimum Wage and Overtime Pay Violations

Minor league players have filed several class action lawsuits against MLB in the same federal trial court where the City of San Jose sued MLB. *Miranda v. Selig* alleges that "reserve clause" rules restricting movement of drafted minor league players between teams for seven years violate antitrust laws.

Minor league players are not unionized. The collective bargaining agreement negotiated by the Major League Baseball Players Association does not apply to them. The "Curt Flood Act" of 1998, which prohibited anti-competitive actions by MLB clubs regarding player contracts, does not apply to them. On September 14, 2015, the trial judge granted MLB's motion to dismiss this case, citing the federal appeals court's decision in the *City of San Jose* case that MLB's antitrust exemption prevents these claims from being litigated.

Senne v. Kansas City Royals Baseball Corp. alleges that MLB violates the federal Fair Labor Standards Act (FLSA), and California, Oregon, Arizona, Florida, Maryland and Pennsylvania laws, by not paying minor leaguers minimum wage and overtime. The *Bridewell v. Cincinnati Reds* decision of the Sixth Circuit U.S. Court of Appeals rejected MLB's defense that these labor laws do not apply to it. MLB had argued that it has seasonal "receipts" that do not meet the test for businesses covered by the FLSA. That case, however, only involved the maintenance staff of Cincinnati's Riverfront Stadium.

Perhaps, the minor leaguers will succeed in this lawsuit before MLB obtains from Congress a statutory exemption from the wage and hour laws for its affiliated minor leagues. On October 20, 2015, the trial judge granted the plaintiffs' motion for certification of their class action in the *Senne* case.

4 - THE FOURTH INNING – CABLE TV BUILDS AND INTERNET LIVE-STREAMING REBUILDS BASEBALL

"No friends, associates, agents, attorneys, guests, or other visitors are allowed access to clubhouse."
-from a Major League Baseball clubhouse door sign

At the Hearing

Judge Marks:

"Wasn't it clear that during this period [from 2012 to 2014] there were discussions about MASN being bought out by another company? ....

In effect, wasn't that the purpose for the long delay in the publication of the arbitration award? ....

Wasn't that the major reason that there was an effort in the Commissioner's office that the Commissioner's office thought that the whole thing could be resolved?....

Didn't that favor, that delay, at least favor the Orioles as much as it favored the Nationals?"

Mr. Weiner (Orioles' lawyer):

"Oh, if it could be sold. Certainly. Certainly. But the payment wasn't in our interest....

If this was an aboveboard transaction, we would have been told about it, we would have been shown this Agreement, we would have – there would have been nothing to hide from us. This [$25 million loan from MLB to the Nationals] was all done behind our back. We never would have agreed to it."

The 20th Century Rise of the Regional and National Broadcasts and Cablecasts of Baseball Games

In 1946, the New York Yankees became the first MLB team to sell, for $75,000, the local television rights to their games. By 2014, the annual rights fees paid by the Yankees-owned regional cable sports network to cablecast Yankee games was $95 million. In 2014, the three highest cablecast rights fees payments were made to the Los Angeles Dodgers ($320 million), the Los Angeles Angels ($150 million) and the Texas Rangers ($150 million).

The rights fees paid by MASN in 2014 to cablecast Orioles and Nationals games were $29 million each. Nineteen of the twenty-eight other MLB teams received higher annual fee payments. The Orioles owner's percentage of ownership of the MASN network was 86% compared to 14% for the Nationals' ownership share. The formula for these percentages was set by the contract between MLB and the Orioles, in return for Peter Angelos's agreement to waive his objections to the Montreal Expos' relocation to Washington, D.C.

In addition to regional cable channel rights fees, each MLB team will receive an equal share of approximately $1.5 billion in national television broadcast and cablecast revenue in 2015, amounting to almost $50 million each.

Wait a minute! In the last chapter, I described the erosion of MLB's marketing skills, because of its unique federal antitrust protection. If MLB is no longer the nation's most popular professional sport (the NFL is #1), and if fewer young Americans are playing or watching the game, then why is television money flooding into the pockets of MLB team owners in increasing amounts?

First, MLB remains the second most popular professional sport in the United States, measured by opinion surveys. It was previously the most popular sport in a nation with a population of 150 million people. It is now the second most popular sport in a nation of 300 million people with far higher disposable incomes than ever before.

Second, because of the greater number of its games and the relative affordability of its ticket prices, Major League Baseball has far more paying spectators than any other sport.

Third, the mass audience for broadcast and cablecast advertisers has been subdivided by the new media of cable television channels, internet streaming video channels, home broadcast and cablecast recording devices, home video games, mobile video games, social media and other electronic diversions. Live sports programming remains a unique environment for mass market advertisers, because of its advantages of 1) its unscripted (and un-previewed) "story lines", 2) the difficulty of recording games for later viewing without commercial interruptions, 3) its appeal to both committed, recurrent fans (for regular season games) and to occasional, casual fans (for post-season playoff games), and 4) its appeal to young, male viewers whom advertisers covet for their disposable income, but who are hard to reach simultaneously in large numbers through other media.

Broadcasts of the NFL Super Bowl championships are the twenty-one most-watched programs in U.S. television history in terms of total audience. For these reasons, television advertisers (through their broadcast and cablecast network brokers) continue to increase their payments to sports team owners, including MLB team owners.

Some team owners have reinvested this flood of television revenues into their teams to compete with the larger market teams, such as those from Los Angeles, New York and Chicago. Other team owners have kept their payrolls low. For example, in some years, the Miami Marlins team payroll has been below the level of its television revenues.

The Virtuous Cycle – Higher Revenues Leads to Playoff Success and to Higher Revenues

Higher-payroll MLB teams have tended to make the post-season playoffs more frequently, and to have more playoff success, than lower-payroll teams. From 1998 to 2015, the post-season results confirm the advantage of having a perennial top ten, or close to top ten, player payroll. These results are even more in favor of higher payroll teams, when it is noted that, although the St. Louis

Cardinals were one of the top ten payroll teams only in 2013, 2012, 2005, 2003, 2001, they never dropped below the fifteen highest payrolls during the 1998 to 2015 period.

From 1995 to 2014, the higher-payroll Yankees (17 times), Red Sox (10 times) and Dodgers (8 times) appeared in the first series of the playoffs frequently, while the lower-payroll Braves (13 times), and Cardinals (12 times) appeared just as frequently. In the second round of the playoffs, the Yankees (10 times) and the Red Sox (6 times) appeared frequently, as did the Cardinals (10 times) and the Braves (6 times). The Yankees (7 times), the higher-payroll Giants (4 times), and the Red Sox (3 times), however, won fourteen league championships, while the lower-payroll Cardinals (4 times) and the Braves (3 times) won only seven league pennants. Finally, the higher-payroll Yankees (5 times), Red Sox (3 times) and Giants (3 times) won eleven World Series championships, while the lower-payroll Cardinals and Miami Marlins won two each.

None of this proves that the team with the highest payroll always wins the World Series. Beginning in 2012, the MLB post-season playoffs were expanded to ten teams by the addition of a one-game playoff between two wild-card teams.

Since 2012, lower-payroll teams have fared almost as well as higher-payroll teams in reaching the post-season playoffs.

Higher-payroll teams are more likely, however, to reap the financial benefits of revenues from higher post-season ticket prices. If a team reinvests its higher regional cable sports network revenue in higher player payrolls, it has an opportunity to create a virtuous cycle of higher box-office and television revenues, leading to greater on-field success, leading to higher box-office and television revenues.

One statistical analysis concludes that none of the twenty teams with the highest relative salaries since 1985 has finished below a .500 season record.

ESPN, Fox and TBS Networks Sign Big Television Contracts With MLB

In 2014, MLB revenues for broadcasts and cablecasts of regular season, playoff and World Series games on the Fox broadcasting network, and the TBS, ESPN and Fox Sports cable channels reached $788.3 million. At their highest values in future years, these contracts will generate $1.5 billion per year in revenue for MLB.

ESPN's contract, from 2014 through 2021, is estimated at a total value of $5.6 billion, or $700 million annually. It grants ESPN the rights to cablecast 90 regular season MLB games, and one Wild Card playoff game, each year.

Fox Sports' contract, from 2014 through 2021, is estimated at a total value of $4 billion, or $500 million annually. It grants Fox Sports the rights to broadcast 52 regular season Saturday games, World Series and All-Star games, one League Championship Series per year, and two Division Series playoffs per year.

TBS's contract, from 2014 through 2021, is estimated at a total value of $2.4 billion, or $300 million annually. It grants TBS the rights to cablecast Sunday afternoon games on the final 13 Sundays of the regular season. It grants TBS the rights to cablecast one League Championship Series, two Division Series playoffs, and one Wild Card game playoff each year.

MLB Network Joins the Cable Sportscasting Game

In 2008, the MLB Network cable channel was launched by Major League Baseball. It is available to almost 70 million households in the U.S. It is approximately one-third owned by its cable and satellite television carriers.

MLB Network carries several out-of-market live broadcasts of games each week. It produces various special programs, documentaries and daily shows, such as MLB Tonight, Hot Stove, Quick Pitch, MLB Now, The Rundown, Intentional Talk, High Heat, Clubhouse Confidential, and MLB Central. In 2012, a separate channel, MLB Strike Zone, similar to NFL Red Zone, launched, showing highlights of all current games, live "look-ins" and updates, all without commercial interruptions.

Because MLB Network is partially owned by cable television providers, it is difficult for it to increase its revenues from subscriber fees paid by those providers. In 2010, its annual revenue was estimated at about $150 million. It has also been placed in some less attractive cable channel positions by its carriers.

MLB Network has the rights to broadcast more than 150 regular season games, and two Division Series games per year. If MLB were paid the same amounts per regular season game by MLB Network that it receives from ESPN, its total revenues would be approximately $1.2 billion per year.

MLB's Great Leap Forward – MLB Advanced Media Streaming Technology Laps the Field

MLB Advanced Media (MLBAM) (soon to be renamed Baseball Advanced Media or "BAM"), runs the internet and web interactive operations of MLB. It runs the official MLB website, and all major league and affiliated minor league club websites. These websites receive an average of four million "hits" per day.

BAM creates and manages the system that sells MLB and affiliated minor league teams' game tickets. BAM bought Tickets.com in 2005 for $66 million. BAM builds mobile apps and games. It provides live audio and video telecasts of most games, and it produces news reports from team-assigned reporters. BAM operates the new instant replay system to review, and confirm or overturn, certain umpire game calls. BAM also owns MLB Radio and BaseballChannel.TV.

BAM was reported to have grossed $620 million in revenue in 2012. It is predicted to earn a profit of $900 million in 2015.

In 2015, the National Hockey League agreed to have BAM run its digital properties and the cable channel NHL Network, including advertising sales, in return for $600 million over six years. The NHL will receive a 10% ownership stake in the planned spin-out of BAM's operations ("BAM Tech") that is tentatively valued at $5 billion.

BAM also provides media services for ESPN, the Professional Golf Association, World Wide Wrestling, CBS Sportsline's March Madness, WatchESPN, and Sony Playstation's Vue Network.

How BAM Became the Internet's Best Live-Streaming Technology

Beginning in 2002, in order to live-stream baseball game telecasts, BAM learned the ins-and-outs of video compression, geo-fencing (to respect home team cable network blackout rights), added information screens for statistics, and multi-device simultaneous delivery. BAM has established regional data centers, and a network of high-speed fiber optic cable connections.

In 2015, the cable channel HBO hired BAM to replace its HBOGo streaming service with the "cable cord-cutting" HBONow internet streaming service, which makes the channel available to subscribers who do not receive cable television.

HBOGo suffered streaming outages during the

season four finale of its *Game of Thrones* program. BAM had proved that it was able to successfully stream the 2014 soccer World Cup championship to a record number of online viewers. HBO had estimated its timeline and cost to build HBONow with internal resources at three years and $900 million. As HBO's contractor, BAM built and launched HBONow in three and a half months for less than $50 million.

BAM initiated its mobile web app, MLB.com, in 2005 with scoreboard, pitch-by-pitch and live audio features. Starting with the launch of the Apple iPhone in 2007, MLB.com became the first live-streaming service technology on many new internet devices, like Roku, Playstation 3, Xbox 360 and Apple TV.

BAM created the AtBat mobile app, which had more than three million downloads by 2012.

BAM operates Statcast, which uses high-speed cameras and radar installed in all MLB stadiums to record each game in three dimensions. From these recordings, a database is built that tracks each motion a player makes. This allows, for example, real-time tracking of player speed and direction that can be compared with historical averages.

BAM has gained a reputation as the best internet live-streaming video service provider. It owns a portfolio of patents, including one for geo-locating fans for live MLB.TV games. It is in a position to compete with Netflix, Hulu, and Amazon as a major live-streaming service specializing in live sports programming. ESPN and Viacom are among the sports programming providers that are looking at BAM as a potential partner, as they consider following younger audiences (and HBO) from cable-only availability to cable and/or internet availability.

MLB is planning to spinoff BAM as a separate company. As such, and with its own (possibly public) stock, the proposed "BAM Tech" would be better positioned than BAM to operate flexibly, to focus on its core expertise of live-streaming, to finance itself, and to attract technical talent with stock options. It might also expand its content beyond sports, to other live entertainment arenas such as music or comedy.

MLB Internet Live-Streaming Revenues and MLB Club Competition

MLB teams have surfed the wave of increasing regional sports cable television revenues in a way that favors the larger television market teams. Some of this imbalance is remedied through MLB revenue sharing and the luxury tax. The larger market teams, however, regularly appear in the lucrative post-season playoff series more often than the smaller market teams.

MLB's foresight in creating its internet live-streaming subsidiary might reduce this imbalance in the future. Local home cablecasts and broadcasts will likely remain off limits from BAM Tech streaming. Nevertheless, the positioning of BAM Tech at the forefront of sports live-streaming packaging and operations provides a new and increasing source of revenue that will be shared equally among all MLB teams. If these added revenues are spent wisely by smaller market teams, they might be at less of a competitive disadvantage.

Revenue sharing and equally divided television revenues have helped increase the competitiveness of small market NFL teams, such as the Green Bay Packers. Expanded NFL playoffs have increased television revenues for, and have maintained fan interest in, teams that previously would have been eliminated from the playoffs with almost half of the season remaining. These same types of reforms could work for baseball.

5 - THE FIFTH INNING – THE ORIOLES AND MLB STICK THE NATIONALS WITH A ONE-SIDED CABLE TELEVISION CONTRACT

"This was a team that had to be moved....We knew it had to relocate. This was a team we were anxious to get rid of."
-Commissioner Allen "Bud" Selig on the relocation of the Montreal Expos to Washington, D.C., in *The Game, Inside the Secret World of Major League Baseball's Power Brokers*

At the Hearing

Mr. Neuwirth (Nationals' lawyer):

"This is supposed to be an inside baseball arbitration. The Orioles knew that. That's why they showed up with Mr. Rifkin. The suggestion that Proskauer was going to have more influence on these arbitrators than Mr. Rifkin is fantasy …. Proskauer was the hired help. Mr. Rifkin was upstairs with the owners. Proskauer was downstairs with the hired help."

A Long, But Easy Road Back to Baseball in Baltimore, and A Long and Hard Road Back to Washington

The relocation of the Montreal Expos franchise to Washington, D.C in 2005 did not require the consent of the Baltimore Orioles majority owner, Peter Angelos, under the territorial rights rules of Major League Baseball. This relocation vote occurred before the 2005 MLB Constitution took effect, and only required the three-quarters approval of National League clubs, and the majority approval of American League clubs, under the 1921 Major League Agreement. Twenty-nine of the thirty MLB clubs voted to approve the relocation.

The St. Louis Browns had to get the consent of the Washington Nationals/Senators owner, Clark Griffith, to move to Baltimore in 1954, because Baltimore was part of the Nationals/Senators' geographic territory. Both teams were in the American League. The 1960 American League Constitution explicitly recognized an exclusive operating territory within a 100-mile radius of a team's home ballpark. It would have placed the entire city of Baltimore in Griffith's territory, if it had applied in 1954.

Clark Griffith never objected to the relocation

of the St. Louis Browns. (Ironically, the Cleveland Browns National Football League team relocated to Baltimore in 1996 to become the Baltimore Ravens.) Until the Baltimore-Washington Parkway opened in 1954, no major highway connected the two cities. The vast majority of each city's population lived within city limits. Travel limitations made the prospect of Washington baseball fans defecting to a Baltimore team a distant prospect.

Baseball game attendance declined in the 1950s as more games were televised. The main relocation consideration for Clark Griffith might have been keeping the Browns franchise alive. Their record of on-field futility had spared the Senators from finishing every year in last place in the eight-team American League. Whatever were his reasons, Griffith consented to the Browns' relocation, and the new Baltimore Orioles relatively quickly became a success in fan attendance and in American League standings.

The Orioles Rise to the Top of the American League Standings From the 1960s Through the 1980s

In the forty-eight years from 1957 to 2005, the Orioles had thirty winning regular season records and eighteen losing season records, including eight consecutive losing records from 1998 to 2005. The Orioles replaced the Yankees as the consistently best American League team in the 1960s through the 1980s. Many of their fans traveled from Washington, D.C. and its suburbs to watch the team play in Baltimore. They also watched their games on television. Their ballpark, Memorial Stadium, was built in 1954, however, and it was located in a residential neighborhood that was accessible only from city streets.

Orioles Park at Camden Yards, in downtown Baltimore, opened in 1992. Besides pioneering the retro-design era of new baseball stadiums, the new ballpark was easily accessible from the Baltimore-Washington Parkway and the Interstate 95 highway. Twenty percent of Orioles fans attending games at the new stadium were estimated to be from Washington, D.C. and its suburbs.

Some of these fans might have traveled to Baltimore only to watch a superior team that won the World Series in 1966, 1970 and 1983. Hall-of-Fame shortstop Cal Ripkin, Jr. played from 1981 to 2001, and won two American League Most Valuable Player awards. He collected 3,184 hits and 431 home runs, played in the All-Star game in nineteen consecutive seasons, and broke New York

Yankees first baseman Lou Gehrig's record for consecutive games played in 1995, ultimately extending his streak to 2,632 games. Playing for the Orioles from 1977 to 1988, and again in 1996, Hall-of-Fame first baseman Eddie Murray eventually collected 3,255 hits and 504 home runs.

Some D.C. area baseball fans would certainly have transferred their interest to a new Washington franchise, if it had arrived in the thirty-four years between the departure of the expansion Senators in 1971 and the arrival of the new Montreal Expos/Washington Nationals in 2005. Although he made his fortune as a lawyer in Washington, D.C., Edward Bennett Williams was the majority owner of the Orioles from 1980 to 1988. His Washington professional connections never developed into support for a new Washington baseball franchise.

The National League expanded by two teams in 1977 (Toronto and Seattle), in 1993 (Miami and Colorado) and in 1998 (Tampa Bay and Arizona). After Peter Angelos became the owner of the Orioles in 1993, he actively discouraged a new or relocated franchise in Washington. As a later member of the executive committee of Major League Baseball, he expressed his opinion that "There are no real baseball fans in D.C." This matched his active efforts to prevent a franchise from relocating to a city where there were, supposedly, no baseball fans anyway.

The High Price for Peter Angelos's Withdrawal of His Threat to Sue MLB for Relocating the Montreal Expos

Peter Angelos's price for the withdrawal of his threat to litigate over the Montreal Expos' 2005 relocation to Washington was high. He received an equal one thirtieth share of the purchase price of $450 million ($15 million) paid in 2006 by the Ted Lerner ownership group to buy the Nationals from Major League Baseball.

The far more important condition for MLB's peace with Peter Angelos, however, was the Agreement of March 28, 2005 for the regional cablecasting of Orioles and Nationals games. The agreement was among MLB, TCR Sports Broadcasting Holding, the new regional cable network created by Angelos, and the Orioles.

In March 2005, the Montreal Expos franchise was owned by the thirty MLB clubs. It had been sold to them for $120 million by Jeffrey Loria in 2003. The club owners and the MLB Commissioner were anxious to sell the Expos, but they needed to move them to a better baseball market in order to get their investment back from a new franchise owner.

On December 3, 2004, MLB formally approved the relocation of the Expos franchise to Washington, D.C. by a vote of 29 to 1. Peter Angelos was the only dissenting owner. Various votes by the District of Columbia [City] Council followed concerning a new city-funded stadium for the franchise. Final approval by the Council for a proposed $440 million stadium (that would eventually cost $770 million) came in a 7-6 vote.

In its September 2004 contract with the District of Columbia to lease Robert F. Kennedy Stadium for the 2005 season, the Montreal Expos represented that they were authorized to enter the agreement "except that the relocation of the franchise ... requires approval from the owners of Major League Baseball clubs in accordance with Baseball Rules and Regulations." There is no mention in the contract of any requirement of consent from the Baltimore Orioles.

As of 2004, it appears that there was no governing MLB Constitution, as there was from June 2005 until December 31, 2012. The National

League had a written Constitution beginning in 1876. The American League had a short written Constitution since 1926. Neither of these documents appear to have addressed franchise relocations into the territory of another team, as the June 2005 MLB Constitution did. Exclusive territory designations were located in separate league rules.

The 1903 "National Agreement for the Government of Professional Baseball Clubs" was an agreement among the National League, the American League and the minor leagues. Article V, Section 1 of the Agreement provided that

> "The circuit of either major league may be changed by transferring either of the above-mentioned franchises to some other city on consent of the majority of the clubs of each major league."

In 1999, Major League Baseball, as the Office of the Commissioner, superseded the separate National League and American League administrative offices, and their league Presidents. From then until the 2005 MLB Constitution was enacted, the revised "Major League Agreement" (MLA) and the "Baseball Rules and Regulations" governed franchise relocations.

The Major League Agreement was the revised agreement that established the Office of the Commissioner in 1921. It is not a public document, but it is reported to have required the following votes to approve a franchise relocation:

"3/4 majority in the affected league, plus a majority of clubs in the other league:.... [for] relocation of a club to a city not within the other league's circuit [transfers into another club's territory require 3/4 majority in both leagues]."

The Major League Agreement reportedly defined the operating territory of the Baltimore Orioles as the city of Baltimore plus

"Anne Arundel, Howard, Carroll and Harford Counties in Maryland."

However these rules are interpreted, they were satisfied by the 29-1 vote of MLB clubs in favor of the Expos' relocation.

Rule 1(c)(2) of the revised March 2008 Major League Rules provides for an MLB club to move into the "home territory" of another MLB club "after approval is obtained under the Major League Constitution." The relocating club must satisfy the

Commissioner of its intention and ability to remain in the new location for a period of five years. Its new stadium must be at least five miles from the stadium of the existing club, and the relocating club

"...shall pay to the Club already located in such home territory such sum of money as the Commissioner deems appropriate under the circumstances.... Any disputes as to the amounts paid as such compensation shall be determined by the Commissioner."

If Peter Angelos had a right in 2004 to object to the Expos' relocation to Washington, D.C. under the MLA or the MLB Rules, as they existed in 2004, it is likely that he would have simply asserted that right. The San Francisco Giants have allegedly asserted against the Oakland Athletics their "home territory" rights to Santa Clara County, as specified in the 2005 MLB Constitution.

If Rule 1(c)(2) had applied in 2004 as it is currently written, however, the Orioles would then only be able to make a claim for compensation from the Commissioner for this territorial intrusion in such amount "as the Commissioner deems appropriate." Without an explicit "home territory" monopoly over Washington, D.C., Peter Angelos was outvoted 29-1 by his fellow owners on relocation.

Peter Angelos was left only with the ability to threaten litigation against MLB for a claim for compensation "as the Commissioner deems appropriate."

Any compensation that might have been awarded to Peter Angelos, after litigation in court, however, would have delayed or destroyed the chance of a smooth relocation of the Expos franchise to Washington, D.C. A lawsuit against the relocation by Peter Angelos also might have invited the scrutiny of the U.S. Congress into the internal affairs of the MLB cartel in a manner that might have threatened its antitrust exemption.

Congressional Hearings on MLB's Antitrust Exemption Make MLB Owners Uncomfortable

The U.S. Senate held hearings in 2002 regarding the MLB antitrust exemption. Among other things, Senators questioned the exercise of MLB's power, through its affiliated minor league teams, to exclude an independent minor league from opening a franchise in Washington, D.C.

Minnesota Senator Mark Dayton stated in the

committee report that

> "Baseball's claimed antitrust exemption also allows the owner of an existing team to prevent another team from being moved to a nearby city where it might 'compete in its market'. One owner wins while depriving, for example, thousands of fans in a city like Washington who want a team and have a willing buyer."

MLB was considering "contracting" the Minnesota Twins and Montreal Expos out of existence during these hearings.

In the Committee Report, Florida Attorney General Robert A. Butterworth expanded the circle of possibly nefarious MLB owners, stating

> "The baseball antitrust exemption allows the various owners of MLB clubs to get together, unlike any other sport, and vote to do away with one or two of their own members so that each remaining member can benefit from the unlucky teams' demise.... Exemption from the law promotes lawlessness.... The result is an 'all-or-nothing' approach, where the clubs band together and impose demands as a collective, leaving cities powerless....

Another result of MLB's cartel behavior condoned by the existence of an antitrust exemption is its dealings with cities without clubs. Existing clubs that are not financially sound are prevented [from] relocating to other locations that could support a club (such as the Washington, D.C. area), so that MLB can retain the city as a threat against other communities who are reluctant to divert crucial funds for local government to the construction of shiny new stadia."

Instead of litigating over the Expos' relocation, Peter Angelos leveraged the possibility of such litigation, and likely Congressional hearings, to extract a regional sports cable channel contract from the MLB owners of the Expos. His fellow MLB owners were liberated from the contract as soon as they sold their ownership shares. The contract would, however, bind the successor franchise owner.

The 2005 Television Contract Drastically Expands the Orioles' "Television Territory"

On March 28, 2005, an agreement was signed by Major League Baseball, TCR Sports Broadcasting Holding, L.L.P. (the operator of the Orioles

Television Network), Baseball Expos, L.L.P. (the Washington Nationals owners at the time), and the Baltimore Orioles Limited Partnership (the "Television Contract"). The fourth paragraph notes that "in December, 2004, the MLB Clubs approved, over the objection of the Orioles, the relocation of the Montreal Expos Baseball Club to Washington, D.C., pursuant to a vote of the member Clubs." The main purposes of the contract were "to resolve various issues" by providing for the cablecasting of Orioles and Nationals baseball games, and by guaranteeing a minimum price for any future sale of the Orioles' franchise.

The entire "Franchise Asset Valuation Protection" provision of the agreement is redacted (blacked out) from the publicly available version of the contract. The minimum guaranteed Orioles franchise future sale price in the agreement has been reported to be $365 million. Given the major increase in the Orioles' franchise value created by its ownership share of the regional sports network revenues allocated by the contract, however, this franchise value protection provision might never become relevant.

In the second paragraph of the contract, the Orioles' home "Television Territory" is defined as "the entire states of Maryland, Virginia, Delaware, the District of Columbia and certain counties in West Virginia, Central Pennsylvania and Eastern North Carolina."

This definition reaches far beyond the Orioles' franchise "operating territory" in the Major League Agreement that existed in 2004, and in the June 2005 MLB Constitution, both of which define it as "City of Baltimore; and Baltimore, Anne Arundel, Howard, Carroll and Harford Counties in Maryland."

Section 2.A of the Television Contract states that

"TCR will be the basis for the regional sports network that will have the sole and exclusive right to present any and all of the Nationals' and the Orioles' baseball games not otherwise retained or reserved by Major League Baseball's national rights agreements."

Section 2.C. excludes radio broadcasting rights from the contract. Section 2.G specifies equal annual "Rights Fees" to be paid by the regional sports network to each team from 2007 through 2011. The fees begin at $25 million and maximize at $29 million.

The 2005 Contract Establishes Procedures for Post-2011 Annual Rights Fees Calculations

Section 2.I of the contract provides for the payment of rights fees after 2011. This was the subject of the 2012 arbitration by the three-owner MLB panel, which was appealed by the Orioles to the New York State Supreme (Trial) Court:

"Future Rights Fees Determination: After 2011, and for each successive five year period, the Orioles, the Nationals and the RSN [regional sports network] first shall negotiate in good faith using the most recent information available which is capable of verification to establish the fair market value of the telecast rights licensed to the RSN for the following five year period."

[Reader Alert – See page 122 for a discussion of what the "duty to negotiate in good faith" requires.]

Section 2.J describes the procedures that must be followed if these good faith negotiations fail:

"Rights Fees Dispute Resolution Mechanism: For any dispute regarding the determination of rights fees pursuant to Subsection 2.I., the dispute resolution mechanism shall be as follows:

2.J.1. Mandatory Negotiation Period: In the event that the Nationals and the RSN, or the Orioles and the RSN, are unable to agree on the fair market value of their respective rights within thirty (30) days or a mutually-agreed upon longer period of time (the "Negotiation Period"), the relevant parties shall follow the procedures set forth in this Subsection to establish the fair market value of the rights licensed to the RSN (the "Rights").

2.J.2. Mediation: In the event that the Nationals and RSN are unable to timely establish the fair market value of the Rights by negotiation as set forth above, then the parties agree to enter into non-binding mediation. The mediation shall be held at a mutually agreeable place and shall be conducted under the auspices of the American Arbitration Association or JAMS.

2.J.3. Appeal: In the event that the Nationals and/or the Orioles and RSN are unable to timely establish the fair market value of the Rights by negotiation and/or mediation as set forth above, then the fair market value of the

Rights shall be determined by the Revenue Sharing Definitions Committee ("RSDC") using the RSDC's established methodology for evaluating all other related party telecast agreements in the industry. The fair market value of the rights established pursuant to this Subsection for the relevant five year period, or such shorter time as may be agreed to by the parties, shall be final and binding on the Nationals and the RSN, and the Nationals and the RSN may seek to vacate or modify such fair market valuation as established by the RSDC only on the grounds of corruption, fraud or miscalculation of figures. Beginning in 2007, the Orioles and the Nationals shall be paid the same rights fees by the RSN.

[Reader Alerts – See page 137 for the Orioles' argument that the MLB arbitration panel failed to apply the "established methodology for evaluating all other related party telecast agreements" in determining the 2012-2016 rights fees award.

See page 141 for the MLB arbitration panel's justification of the "established methodology" that it applied.

See page 179 for Judge Marks's questioning

of what "established methodology" means in this contract.]

2.J.4. The above-described dispute resolution mechanism shall be applied unless otherwise agreed to by the RSN and MLB on or before June 1, 2005."

Section 2.L of the contract provides that rights fees distributions "shall be made consistent with the parties' relative and then-applicable partnership profits interest in the RSN." Section 2.N. provides

"Equity Interest In Regional Sport Network: The Major League Baseball Partner (as defined below) shall initially receive a 10% partnership profits interest in TCR. Following the full completion of the fifth year of operation of the RSN, the Major League Baseball Partner, or its assignee, shall receive an annual increase of its partnership profits interest at the rate of one percentage point per year, until such time as the initial interest and the annual increases to its profits interests total 33% ..."

Section 2.P of the contract provides

"2.P.1. In consideration for the receipt of the equity interests in TCR, referred to in Subsection N above, the Major League Baseball Partner shall contribute the sum of $75,000,000 as its capital contribution to TCR, and BOLP shall contribute the Orioles' rights relating to its Television Territory as its capital contribution to TCR. At such time as the Major League Baseball Partner's capital contributions are made, it shall receive credit in its capital account for the amount of the payment. As a result of its capital contribution, BOLP shall receive a capital account credit of $150,000,000....

2.P.3. TCR shall utilize the cash capital referred to in Subsection 2.P.1. above for such capital expenditures and operational costs as are necessary to conduct its operations."

The 2005 Contract Establishes Penalties for Failure to Pay the Annual Rights Fees

Section 2.R of the contract provides

"Remedies For Non-Payment; Insolvency: In the event that the RSN does not pay either the Orioles or the Nationals the rights fees contemplated herein in a timely fashion, then:

2.R.1. The RSN shall have a right to cure such non-payment within a reasonable period of time after written notice of the non-payment from either the Nationals or the Orioles, as the case may be. Such time shall not exceed 30 days.

2.R.2. If payment is not made within the applicable cure period, then the Orioles and/or the Nationals, as appropriate, shall have a right to seek money damages or avail themselves of any other appropriate remedies that may be available for such non-payment, including without limitation, termination of the license to their respective telecast rights granted herein; provided, that they will not terminate such licenses until thirty days after the expiration of the cure period set forth in Subsection 2.R.1 above. Such termination shall take effect upon receipt by the RSN of a written notice of termination (the "Notice of Termination")....

[Reader Alerts – See page 134 for the Nationals' July 3, 2014 letter to the RSN giving notice of its impending right to terminate the 2005 Television Contract, because of the RSN's failure to pay the appropriate amount of 2012-2016 cablecast

rights fees.

See page 136 for the RSN's court motion to enjoin the Nationals from terminating the 2005 Television Contract.

See page 139 for Judge Marks's August 21, 2014 order preventing the Nationals from terminating the contract.]

2.R.4. Notwithstanding any other provision of this Agreement, upon receipt of the Notice of Termination or at any time thereafter, the RSN has the right to and may seek any and all immediate legal or equitable relief and remedies from such termination available in any court of law with jurisdiction, including, without limitation, the right to seek injunctive relief or specific performance. In the instance in which there are no other material defaults of this Agreement, other than the delinquent payment of rights fees, and the Nationals or the Orioles, as applicable, have not been materially prejudiced by the delinquent payment, payment of the delinquent rights fees plus interest at any time prior to the final determination of a court of original jurisdiction pursuant to this Subsection shall constitute a cure of such default, and the termination, if any, shall be void and of no effect. Multiple violations of the failure to pay rights fees shall be considered a rebuttable presumption of material prejudice."

The 2005 Contract Establishes the Procedures to Take Rights Fees Disputes to Arbitration by the MLB Commissioner

Section 8 of the contract, "Dispute Resolution" provides that, except regarding certain provisions such as the "Rights Fees Dispute Resolution Mechanism", and procedures for contract termination after the rights fees are delinquent in payment, the Orioles, the Nationals and the RSN can take their disputes with each other, under the contract, to the Commissioner as a sole arbitrator after mediation. Any disputes between the Orioles or the RSN and MLB are to be taken to a commercial arbitration provider.

The agreement does not establish a time limitation for its existence. In exchange for making the agreement, the Orioles released "any and all claims ... arising prior to the execution of this Agreement related to the relocation of the Montreal Expos Baseball Club to Washington, D.C."

The agreement was signed by Peter Angelos for

the Baltimore Orioles and TCR Sports Broadcasting, by Allen H. (Bud) Selig, the MLB Commissioner, as agent for the MLB Clubs, and by Robert DuPuy for Baseball Expos, L.P.

6 - THE SIXTH INNING – WHAT DOES THAT CLAUSE MEAN?

Joe Hardy: "I want to exercise the escape clause which is to take place on the twenty-fourth, which is today."
Mr. Applegate: "Well now. Aren't you being a little hasty?"
Joe Hardy: "I've thought it all over. I found out there's something more important in life than being a hero."
Mr. Applegate: "Deep, this boy. Very deep."
Joe Hardy: "I want out. I wanna go back."
-from *Damn Yankees*, the Broadway musical/film

At the Hearing

Mr. Neuwirth (Nationals' lawyer):

"But what we know from the documents that have now been produced is that what Mr. Rifkin was doing behind the scenes was working to prevent this award from ever being released to try to pressure the Nationals to make a deal....

[I]t is remarkable – remarkable -- that MASN

Copyright © George Abbott and Douglass Wallop, excerpted from the book of the play *Damn Yankees* and/or the screenplay of the 1958 film *Damn Yankees* and used here with express permission of the copyright owners. All Rights Reserved.

and the Orioles have had the gumption to tell your Honor what they have said about this $25 million payment.

In this e-mail to Mr. Rifkin, Mr. Manfred says: '…we have invested $25 million to buy time.' Just as your Honor noted. There was no trick here. This was done because the Orioles were trying to pressure the Nationals to make a deal that the Orioles wanted that was going to let them get a billion dollars of value out of MASN ….

Mr. Manfred described the terms that MLB and Mr. Rifkin were discussing, which include…. 'We understand that the agreement [to sell MASN] would have to eliminate any possibility of issuing the current RSDC opinion.' In other words, the Nationals were not going to get what they were entitled to."

MLB Expos Owners Assign Their 2005 Television Contract to the New Washington Nationals Owners

The March 2005 television contract was signed by "Baseball Expos, L.P. d/b/a/ [doing business as] Washington Nationals Baseball Club." At the time the contract was signed, Baseball Expos, L.P.

[limited partnership] was owned by all the MLB clubs. Ted Lerner and his family did not buy the Nationals franchise until July 24, 2006. Section 11.C of the contract, however, provides that

> "This Agreement and the terms contained herein irrevocably are binding upon and shall inure to the benefit of the parties and their respective successors and permitted assigns ...
> provided that in the event that either the Orioles, the Nationals or the RSN are sold, conveyed, assigned or in any other way transferred, in whole or in part, all subsequent purchaser(s), assignees or transferees shall be unconditionally bound to all terms and conditions of this Agreement."

This means that when the Lerner family bought the Nationals franchise from MLB in 2006 for $450 million, they became bound to the television contract that MLB had negotiated with Peter Angelos. Under contract law, rights under a contract can be assigned to someone who was not an original contract party. Duties under a contract can be delegated to a party that was not an original contract party.

In this case, the Lerner family knew that the one-sided television deal that MLB had signed with

Peter Angelos was an additional cost of their purchase of the Nationals. But the annual "rights fees" part of the contract only specified the fees that would be paid through 2011. What was expected to happen after that?

The Duty to Negotiate Post-2011 Rights Fees in Good Faith

Section 2.I of the contract requires that

> "After 2011, and for each successive five year period, the Orioles, the Nationals and the RSN first shall negotiate in good faith using the most recent information available which is capable of verification to establish the fair market value of the telecast rights licensed to the RSN for the following five year period."

State "common law" (judge-made case law) of contracts, and state statutory law on contracts for the sale of goods, recognizes that "Every contract imposes upon each party a duty of good faith and fair dealing in its performance and its enforcement." There is no general contract requirement of good faith/fair dealing, however, regarding the negotiation of a contract. This is for practical and technical reasons.

The practical reason is that it is difficult to impose a contract duty on a negotiating party before the actual contract is created. American law generally takes a "buyer beware" approach to contract negotiations. Each party is free to negotiate the most favorable terms for itself that it can. Special reasons must exist in order for the law to step into the contract negotiations phase to impose protections against superior negotiating power or skill.

In the 1940s, European legal scholars brought into the U.S. statutes on the sale of goods the concept of "unconscionability". In part, this was a defense to contract enforcement that relieved a party from contract performance if the contract terms "shocked the conscience." In addition, or alternatively in some states, a party was relieved from performance if the procedures for contract formation involved oppression or unfair surprise by one party against another. The defense of unconscionability has declined in importance, however, as more state and federal consumer protection statutes have been enacted.

The technical reason that no general duty to *negotiate* in good faith exists in U.S. contract law is that if a negotiating party induces another party to enter a contract through a misrepresentation, the wronged party can sue under tort/personal injury law for damages (and can recover more money than is possible under contract law). Continental European law does not allow negotiators to sue for personal injury in this manner. The duty of good faith in contract negotiations takes its place.

Peter Angelos, and the MLB lawyers who drafted the 2005 television contract, probably understood that there could be no real enforcement of the contract term that the parties "shall negotiate in good faith" the post-2011 television rights fees. They put it in the contract anyway.

The Post-2011 Rights Fees Arbitration by the MLB Revenue Sharing Definitions Committee to Determine "Fair Market Value"

Section 2.J of the Television Contract describes the "Dispute Resolution Mechanism" that both parties are expected to follow. After a mandatory thirty day negotiation period (or longer if mutually agreed), if a mutual determination of the "fair market value" of the television rights fees is not agreed to, the parties are to enter a non-binding mediation. A mediation is a negotiation facilitated by a neutral third party mediator.

If the required mediation does not resolve the

rights fees dispute over "fair market value" (which is very likely if it is non-binding), a "Revenue Sharing Definitions Committee" (RSDC) of three MLB owners is required to use its "established methodology for evaluating all other related party telecast agreements in the industry" to determine the appropriate telecast rights fees dollar amount. This determination

> "shall be final and binding on the Nationals and the RSN, and the Nationals and the RSN may seek to vacate or modify such fair market valuation as established by the RSDC only on the grounds of corruption, fraud or miscalculation of figures."

This part of the contract essentially creates a binding arbitration process in which a three-member panel of arbitrators (the RSDC) determines the fair market value of the rights fees in a private, non-judicial forum. The arbitration result can then be appealed to a court only on the specified grounds of arbitrator corruption, fraud in the arbitration process or faulty mathematics.

A Short History of Mandatory Arbitration Contract Clauses

Arbitration is a legal procedure that has grown

in importance in the U.S. economy since the 1970s. It has been permitted, as an alternative to litigation in court, since the enactment of the Federal Arbitration Act in 1925. For many years, arbitration was limited to the labor law field of labor-management disputes. Beginning in the 1980s, however, companies began requiring mandatory arbitration of disputes in consumer contracts.

In part, mandatory consumer arbitration was imposed by businesses as a response to the growth of the consumer contract defense of unconscionability. In part, it was a business reaction to the wave of consumer protection statutes in the 1970s. Most importantly, however, it was a business reaction to the growth of class action litigation on behalf of consumers.

A class action allows the similar contract (or personal injury or statutory) claims of many different consumers or businesses, to be consolidated into one case. This consolidation makes it worthwhile for skilled litigators (like Peter Angelos) to sue for individual injuries or contract breaches that, from the plaintiffs' lawyer's perspective, might not be worth suing for in separate cases.

If a lawyer can sue for hundreds or thousands of

injured parties in one case, the lawyer's "contingent fee" percentage share of a monetary judgment (if there is one) might make him rich, while his injured clients are also compensated. Most class actions take years to litigate, however. The plaintiffs' lawyers usually receive nothing for their time spent before they obtain a favorable judgment. So few, if any, plaintiffs' lawyers "get rich quick".

Many mandatory arbitration clauses in consumer contracts prohibit class action lawsuits. The Consumer Financial Protection Bureau (CFPB) was created by the Dodd-Frank Act's reform of the financial industry, after the Wall Street Crash of 2008. The Dodd-Frank Act requires the CFPB to study the fairness of mandatory consumer arbitration clauses in financial contracts, and to determine whether they should be regulated or prohibited.

There are several reasons, however, why businesses and consumers might prefer arbitration over lawsuits as a method of resolving legal disputes. First, the arbitration process is usually faster than litigation in court. This is because judges often handle all kinds of criminal and civil cases, while arbitrators usually resolve only specialized business matters. Second, specialized arbitrators (who are often retired judges) often have a greater expertise in the subject of the arbitration than judges have, and can be selected by the parties based on their expertise. Third, because arbitration takes less time than litigation, it can be less expensive. Fourth, the terms of many mandatory consumer arbitration contract clauses provide that the party requiring arbitration will pay the legal and other costs of the other party, up to a certain amount.

Consumers and their advocates, however, often object to mandatory arbitration for several reasons. First, the results of an arbitration are usually confidential, so that even if a consumer wins, his winning arguments cannot be the basis for another arbitration or litigation by a future consumer. Second, the location where the arbitration must occur is usually where the business is located, which might be inconvenient for the consumer. Third, there is no jury trial right in arbitration. Fourth, there is no class action right in arbitration (although some arbitration providers say that they will provide for class arbitrations). Fifth, small claims courts are quick, and inexpensive litigation forums for consumers that should not be prohibited by a mandatory arbitration clause. They have streamlined procedures that do not require lawyer involvement. (Businesses are often represented by their lawyers in small claims court, however, and bring more cases to small claims courts than consumers do.)

The Nationals (Allegedly) Tear Up the MASN Rights Fees Proposal, and the RSDC Arbitration of the Nationals-RSN Rights Fees Dispute Begins

In accordance with the "negotiation first, mediation second, arbitration third" procedures for setting the fair market value of television rights in Sections 2.J.1 and 2.J.2 of the 2005 contract, the RSN (later renamed "Mid-Atlantic Sports Network" or "MASN") hired a consultant to produce a five-year telecast rights fees proposal. MASN presented it to the Nationals.

According to MASN,

"... representatives of the Nationals ... summarily rejected the proposal by literally tearing it to pieces…. The meeting came to an abrupt end, and the parties initiated arbitration before the RSDC ["Revenue Sharing Definitions Committee"] as provided for in Section 2.J.3 …"

Both parties felt that the next step of mediation would be a waste of time. They waived it.

On June 30, 2014 (after being delayed two years while MLB tried to sell MASN to an outside investor), the RSDC issued its arbitration award determining the fair market value of the television rights fees. The Committee was composed of the President of the Pittsburgh Pirates, the Principal Owner of the Tampa Bay Rays, and the owner of the New York Mets. The staff of MLB, including the future Commissioner Rob Manfred, administered the arbitration.

The RSDC determined that the fair market value of the MASN television rights fees for the Nationals from 2012 to 2016 would be

2012: $53,170,018 - 2013: $56,253,879
2014: $59,347,843 - 2015: $62,611,974
2016: $66,744,364.

MASN had argued that the fees for this period should be $34 million for each year.

The Orioles Petition the New York Court to Vacate the MLB Arbitration Award

On July 2, 2014, MASN sued in the New York Supreme (Trial) Court in Manhattan to vacate or modify the RSDC arbitration decision of June 30, 2014. On July 7, the Nationals filed a petition with the MLB Commissioner for him to confirm the RSDC arbitration award.

On July 24, 2014, the Nationals also filed a petition with the court for it to confirm the RSDC arbitration award. The Nationals' petition to the court criticized the MLB Commissioner for failing to confirm the RSDC award upon the Nationals' request, and for failing to impose any sanction on MASN for appealing the award to a court. It alleged that this failure was contrary to a June 30, 2014 letter to the Nationals "that he [the Commissioner] would sanction either party if it commenced a litigation related to the RSDC decision." Because the Commissioner would not confirm the award, and MASN would not pay the award, the Nationals sued to have the award enforced by the court.

The e-mail letter from Commissioner Selig to Ted Lerner and Peter Angelos dated June 30, 2014 stated, in part,

> "I am deeply saddened by the fact that you have not been able to resolve amicably the pending broadcast rights dispute…. As you are well aware, we have expended hundreds of hours and extensive resources in an effort to reach an accommodation that preserves the massive and inherent value of MASN for the benefit of both

Clubs. Unfortunately, these efforts have come to naught solely due to your unfathomable inability to agree on a fair division of value. In my view, neither of you has approached this negotiation with the best interest of the game paramount in your mind....

Both the Orioles and the Nationals have at various times made threats to institute litigation in connection with this dispute, despite my office's extended, good-faith efforts to have this matter resolved by agreement. On a personal note, I owned a Club for decades and I can honestly say that under no circumstances would I have threatened, let alone commenced, litigation against Baseball....

I hope that you both will put your parochial interest to one side and work with my office to reach an agreement."

The 2005-2011 rights fees payments were alleged by the Nationals to be "substantially below market value" in order to induce the Orioles' cooperation in the franchise movement to Washington. While negotiations and arbitration of fees for the succeeding five-year period dragged on, the payments for the 2012 and 2013 seasons were also allegedly "far below the fair market value of the

Nationals' telecast rights as determined in the RSDC Award."

The Nationals' lawyers' letter to MASN claims that "the RSDC Decision requires MASN to pay the Nationals an additional $10,037,204.50 for the telecast rights fee payments due on April 1, 2014 and June 1, 2014 of this year." A July 3, 2014 letter from the Nationals' lawyers to the MASN lawyers gave notice that "Failure by MASN to cure its defaults by August 6, 2014 shall trigger the Nationals rights under Section 2.R of the ... Agreement to seek all appropriate remedies for nonpayment, including ... termination of MASN's license to telecast Nationals games." The Orioles' lawsuit in the New York court was characterized by the Nationals as being "for the apparent purpose of further delaying MASN's payment of the fair market value of the Nationals' telecast fee rights."

The Orioles/MASN lawyers responded in a letter to the Commissioner dated July 8, stating for the first time that

> "Critically relevant is also the fact that the Commissioner and Baseball have a direct financial interest in confirming the RSDC Decision. Not only does Baseball have approximately a 34% financial interest in every

dollar steered toward telecast rights fees and away from MASN's profits under the Revenue Sharing Plan, but also, in 2013 – over a year before the RSDC Decision was issued – the Commissioner privately paid $25 million to the Nationals, entering into an agreement with that Club, through which Baseball would recoup those funds from the monies to be paid under the RSDC award at issue here. We understand that Baseball borrowed $25 million from its credit facility to give to the Nationals and that Baseball has an obligation to repay those funds in short order. We further understand that no provision was made in the arrangement with the Nationals for the recoupment of those funds other than through the additional telecast rights fees in the RSDC's disputed award. As such, the Commissioner and Baseball have a financial interest in recouping their $25 million through confirmation of the RSDC Decision.

In light of these facts ... any further action by the Commissioner regarding this matter would be inherently biased, prejudicial, and tainted.... MASN's action will advance claims of misconduct, including improper private arrangements, illicit promises and representations, unacceptable conflicts of interest, and other wrongful conduct and actions in which the Commissioner and MLB regrettably were active participants. Those, and other improper actions, corrupted the RSDC process and led to the RSDC's contrived and fraudulent decision."

The Orioles Move for an Injunction to Stop the Nationals From Terminating the Television Contract

On August 13, 2014, MASN filed a Motion for a Preliminary Injunction by the court to order the Nationals to not terminate or interfere with the rights of MASN to telecast their games. In order to receive the injunction, MASN had to allege facts showing it would be likely to succeed in vacating the MLB arbitration award. MASN alleged that

"MASN has established that it is likely to succeed in vacating the RSDC award because of pervasive conflicts of interest, intolerable self-dealing and fraud that thoroughly infected and completely undermined any semblance of the fair and objective arbitral process ... Major League Baseball, its hand-picked arbitrators, and the Nationals shared not only counsel but also a financial interest in doing everything possible to undermine the promises memorialized in the [television contract], including the promise to compensate the Orioles and MASN for the loss of almost a third of their market share, business and business opportunities, and their exclusivities in the Orioles television territory. They did so, over MASN's repeated and strenuous objections, by rigging the RSDC proceeding to reach a pre-determined result....

MASN also has shown that it will suffer irreparable harm if the Nationals are permitted to terminate MASN's right to broadcast Nationals games, especially in the middle of the baseball season ..."

MASN argued further that the court was not limited to a review of the arbitration award only for "corruption, fraud or miscalculation of figures." It argued that under the Federal Arbitration Act, the court could also vacate the award for "manifest disregard of the law, ... evident partiality; prejudicial misconduct; or an *ultra vires* [unauthorized] or flawed execution of the arbitrators' powers."

Regarding the substance of its allegations, MASN alleged that

"The RSDC members themselves – representatives of Major League Clubs that receive large amounts of revenue sharing money from more financially successful clubs - had a vested interest in diverting money from MASN's profits into telecast rights fees, because a substantial portion of those fees are diverted to revenue-sharing beneficiaries such as the Pittsburgh Pirates and Tampa Bay Rays. In addition, the same law firm that represented the Nationals in the arbitration also represented the clubs of all three RSDC members and Baseball itself while the RSDC arbitration was pending and failed to fully disclose those obvious conflicts of interest. Moreover, the RSDC simply refused to apply the established methodology for determining the fair market value of the teams' telecast rights, which Baseball agreed to do in the [television contract] …. And Baseball … never instructed the RSDC to use the 'established methodology' nor took any steps to cure the process or the decision. Instead, Baseball furthered its own economic self-interest by approving a process that jettisoned the promised 'established methodology' and simply 'backed into' the greater amount of telecast fees that MLB wanted MASN to pay—and, perhaps promised MASN would pay—to the Nationals."

Regarding its allegation of improper

participation in the arbitration by the Nationals' law firm, Proskauer Rose, which had, in other matters, advised the Nationals, MLB and the clubs of the three RSDC members, MASN argued that

> "MASN persistently objected, demanded more information, and even moved to disqualify the firm, only to be rebuffed at every turn. MASN was kept largely in the dark about the unseemly web of relationships that infected and compromised the arbitral process with conflicts of interest, partiality and self-dealing....
>
> During the course of the RSDC arbitration and before any award was issued ... Proskauer was representing everyone in the room—except, of course, MASN and [the Orioles]. And MASN and [the Orioles] timely and repeatedly objected to that fact."

On August 21, 2014, Judge Marks officially granted the MASN motion for a preliminary injunction to prevent the Nationals from terminating or interfering with the Orioles' telecast rights under the contract.

7 - THE SEVENTH INNING – THE RIGHTS FEES DISPUTE GOES INTO OVERTIME

Mr. Applegate: "Look Lola. Here's the tie up. This is a mass torture deal, like the Thirty Years War. I've got thousands of Washington fans drooling under the illusion that the Senators are gonna win the pennant."
Lola: "Aw chief, that's awfully good. When they lose there'll be suicides, and heart attacks and apoplexy. Just like the good old days."
-from *Damn Yankees*, the Broadway musical/film

At the Hearing

Mr. Neuwirth (Nationals' lawyer):

"Bloomberg in 2013 valued the Orioles at $1.12 billion when factoring in the team's majority stake in regional sports network MASN. That amount, in fact, is very consistent with the projections of rights fees that the Nationals made, and it is completely inconsistent with what were truly the lowball numbers that MASN and the Orioles put forth.

Copyright © George Abbott and Douglass Wallop, excerpted from the book of the play *Damn Yankees* and/or the screenplay of the 1958 film *Damn Yankees* and used here with express permission of the copyright owners. All Rights Reserved.

And why is MASN pushing – why are the Orioles pushing so hard on the Nationals to make a deal? Because they want to cash out that value and force the Nationals, who are strapped for cash, to participate in that because they won't have any other way to get the cash …."

The Normal Business of the MLB Revenue Sharing Definitions Committee

According to its arbitration decision, the normal function of the MLB Revenue Sharing Definitions Committee ("RSDC")

"... is to hear appeals from Clubs regarding the proper treatment of certain transactions – most frequently transactions between Clubs and related parties – for purposes of Major League Baseball's Revenue Sharing Plan ("Plan"). The primary purpose of this review is to ensure that Clubs do not divert revenue that should be covered by the Plan…. The RSDC does not normally arbitrate disputes between and among Clubs and networks. However, … under the Agreement the Orioles, Nationals and MASN mutually selected the RSDC to serve as the sole arbitrator of any disputes regarding the fair market value of the Clubs' broadcast rights …"

The RSDC Analyzes the MASN Rights Fees Valuation Dispute

In the 2012 arbitration by the RSDC, the Nationals argued that the fair market value of their telecast rights for the year 2012 was $109 million, while MASN argued that those rights were worth $34 million. The RSDC read the opinions of each party's expert witnesses and the parties' written arguments, and it heard their oral arguments.

The RSDC began its explanation of its decision with a description of how it determines the fair market value of related party transactions for MLB's revenue sharing plan. The RSDC referred to its methodology as the "Bortz approach", because the RSDC uses Bortz Media & Sports Group as its consultants for its revenue sharing plan analysis. This analysis includes revenues and expenses of the relevant party, and "comparisons of the Club's local rights fees with verified fees of Clubs in comparable Major League markets."

In explaining its decision, the RSDC stated that

"This Committee in its prior estimates of the fair market value of broadcasting rights has considered, in addition to the network's income statement, a myriad of factors that may influence the value of the Club's rights [such as telecast ratings, media regulation, television industry changes, and equitable considerations such as reliance on existing telecast contracts]."

Contrary to the methodology requested by the Nationals, which would be primarily a "comparable markets" analysis,

"While the RSDC has considered market comparables as a "check" or point of reference in considering the results of the income statement analysis in the past, it has never relied exclusively or even predominantly on comparables in determining whether a rights fee is of fair market value ... because each market is unique.... We [apply the Committee's established methodology] to the dispute at issue by (i) conducting a pro forma analysis of MASN (which involves projecting MASN's revenues and expenses to determine an appropriate rights fee), (ii) considering comparable local rights fee agreements for purposes of verifying the pro forma analysis, and (iii) evaluating other factors raised by the parties in the proceeding that may impact the value of the local broadcasting rights of the Nationals."

The RSDC's Valuation of the Nationals' Rights Fees Based on MASN Projected Revenues and Typical RSN Profit Margins

The first part of the RSDC's valuation of the Nationals' 2012-2016 telecast rights fees proceeded in two steps: 1) an estimate of MASN's projected operating profit for this period, before rights fees distributions, and 2) an estimate of MASN's operating margin to "back into" the total rights fees it can distribute.

MASN projected its 2012-2016 revenues using its 2012 revenue estimate of $163,670,481. It assumed its growth at between 6 and 7 percent, and projected eventual 2016 revenues of $205,543,441. MASN's revenues grew at a compounded rate of 7.3 percent from 2008-2011. The Nationals did not submit to the Committee an alternative projection of MASN 2012-2016 revenues.

The RSDC assumed that 95% of MASN's revenues come from Orioles and Nationals baseball programs, to which 90% of its costs were attributable. (Football and college sports programs were responsible for 10%.) This left $114,114,384 in operating profit (before rights fees) for 2012.

The RSDC predicted that MASN's 33% operating profit margin in 2011 would decline thereafter, because the rights fees set in the original contract were below comparable rights fees paid by regional sports networks for Cleveland Indians, Atlanta Braves and Texas Rangers telecasts. The margins were predicted to decrease with higher rights fees during the second five-year rights fees period.

Negative operating margins were reported for the Texas Rangers regional sports network in 2007. The Committee's opinion was that MASN's operating profit margin would be zero "if the entire game and studio production costs for the Nationals and Orioles are added to the ninety percent of MASN's non-production operating expenses attributable to baseball programming."

Then the Committee addressed an argument by the Orioles that became a major point of contention in the later appeal of the RSDC's decision in the New York court.

"While Bortz Media has assumed in prior evaluations conducted for the Committee that broadcasters operate at a margin that typically does not exceed twenty percent, the Committee has never accepted that the assumption of a twenty-percent operating margin is reasonable for all regional sports networks in all markets and in all circumstances. In the context of a *retrospective* review of the operating results under a related party agreement, the twenty-percent operating margin is a rough line of demarcation between agreements that are likely of fair market value (*i.e.*, a twenty-percent operating margin or below) and those that require additional scrutiny because the operating margin of the broadcaster is higher than the norm (*i.e.*, greater than twenty percent). But the RSDC has never adopted a bright line rule that broadcasters will not enter into rights fee agreements that would reduce their operating margin below twenty percent. To the contrary, as noted above, Bortz Media has concluded that a number of local broadcast agreements were of fair market value even though the regional sports network reported operating margins well below the twenty percent figure. *See generally, e.g.*, Texas Bortz Report; Cleveland Bortz Report. Furthermore, none of the related party regional sports networks evaluated by Bortz Media in the past was based on a business model that required the payment of rights fees to two MLB franchises (with no other professional sports programming during the baseball off-season)."

In evaluating "what fair market operating margin is appropriate for MASN in 2012", the

Committee first noted that

"... an important source of compensation under the Agreement is the equity value in MASN, which, in turn, is based on its operating margin. In this regard, the Agreement has provided the Orioles with significant returns. According to MASN's own data, the operating margin for the entire network was 6.2% in 2007, and grew to 25.7% in 2008, 25.1% in 2009, 30.9% in 2010 and 33.4% in 2011."

The Committee rejected the Orioles' argument that it should be guaranteed a twenty-percent operating margin by stating that

"MASN and the Orioles effectively contend that the RSDC should simply calculate rights fees by examining revenues and expenses and then ensuring MASN a twenty-percent operating margin. If the parties to the Agreement had intended this mechanical approach, it would have been simple to write the contract language to capture that intention. The parties to the Agreement chose not to do that."

The Committee rejected the Nationals' argument that it should receive $109 million for its 2012 rights fees by stating that

"If the Nationals' valuation of their rights fees at approximately $109 million in 2012 were accepted, MASN would be unprofitable if it paid the Orioles a rights fee of more than $11 million (which, itself, would constitute a 62% reduction from the $29 million rights fee that the Orioles received in 2011.) Thus, the Nationals' contention that it would receive a rights fee of $109 million in an arm's length transaction with MASN cannot be accepted by the Committee because MASN would not agree to a rights fee that would potentially bankrupt the network."

Returning to its rejection of the Orioles' argument for a twenty-percent operating margin, the Committee stated

"First, as a matter of contract, the parties agreed that the Nationals' rights fee would be adjusted upward in 2012 to "fair market value," which, considering the realities of the current market for local rights, almost certainly requires a reduction in MASN's operating margin.... It is impossible to ignore the fact that the market value of live sports programming has increased substantially in recent years.... As the price of rights fees has increased over the last few years, the margins of the regional sports networks – which are not typically able to fully pass on the increased expenses to cable distributors – have, not surprisingly, decreased. The Agreement also provides that the Orioles would get the same rights fee adjustment, regardless of the relative value of the Orioles' rights. The parties' agreement that the Orioles will receive the same rights fee as the Nationals, even if the Orioles' rights would be worth less in an arm's length transaction, means that the operating margin of MASN presumably would be lower than the average RSN where a Club is required to negotiate its rights fees independently.

Taking these considerations into account, the Committee believes that MASN would have been forced to operate at a relatively low operating margin for baseball programming in 2012 if the rights fees for the Nationals were obtained in an arm's length negotiation. In 2007, MASN's operating margin for the entire network was only 6.2% despite the fact that the Nationals' broadcasting rights were far less valuable than they are today because of changes in the market. Indeed, in light of the robust market for sports rights fees in 2012, MASN's contractual obligation to increase the Nationals' rights fee to fair market value in 2012, and the

THE RIGHTS FEES DISPUTE GOES INTO OVERTIME

corresponding right of the Orioles to receive the same fee as the Nationals, it would be wholly unrealistic to assume that MASN could recognize an operating margin much higher than the six percent network operating margin it achieved in 2007. Accordingly, the Committee will assume that MASN would have achieved an operating margin from baseball programming in 2012 of five percent had it obtained the Nationals local broadcast rights in an arm's length transaction....

At a five percent operating margin, MASN would pay a combined $106,340,036 in rights fees to the Nationals and Orioles ... the Nationals and Orioles would each receive $53,170,018 in rights fees for 2012. We believe that the Nationals rights fees should increase during the period at the same rate that MASN's revenues are projected to grow, which would result in rights fees for the Nationals of $56,253,879 in 2013, $59,347,843 in 2014, $62,611,974 in 2015, and $66,744,364 in 2016.

We must point out that even accepting MASN's conservative projection of its revenue growth, the network's operating margin will increase over the five-year period to approximately eight percent on baseball programming by 2016, and to eleven percent overall. However, MASN will have the opportunity to achieve an even more significant improvement in its operating margin because, unlike many RSNs which are locked into long-term affiliate agreements, a substantial percentage of MASN's affiliate agreements expire prior to 2016. To the extent MASN is able to enter affiliate agreements that exceed its projections based on the increased popularity of the Nationals and Orioles, or other factors, MASN's profitability will increase."

The RSDC's Projections of MASN Income Based on Comparable Contracts

The Committee members then began their analysis of MASN's future income by rejecting a comparison of similar regional sports network telecast contract rights proposed by the Nationals and MLB. They described the Nationals' and MLB's "comparables" as "deficient in material respects", such as absence of verifiable contract terms, and a mismatch between the periods of time covered by the similar contracts and the 2012-2016 period.

The Committee members also rejected the Orioles' proposed contract comparisons, as "results-oriented rather than realistic." Further,

"MASN's ... analysis lumps its four comparables into a single number: the average of aggregated rights income per average aggregated game per average aggregated DMA household.... Layering together a daisy chain of undifferentiated aggregate averages does not produce a sufficiently precise comparable to assess the Nationals' individuated fair market value.... The probative limitations of MASN's aggregated averages are not just theoretical. The 2012 rights fees of the Rangers, Astros, Marlins, and Rays range from $42,654,057 (Rangers) to $14,734,000 (Rays). If this was an internally coherent group of comparables, we would expect to see much narrower variance in fees."

The Committee members described their methodology, as

"We ... exclude the Dodgers from the comparable group [because its contract terms were only hypothetical]. We also normalize the rights fees contained in the comparable agreements identified by the parties by discounting back to 2012 according to each contract's average annualized growth, and by making no assumptions about 2011-2012 growth beyond what the actual contract terms provide...."

Thus, when properly valued…. the income-statement analysis produced rights fees for the five-year period that are roughly in between the rights fees obtained by each party's identified comparables."

The RSDC then concluded

"Why, then, are MASN's bid and the Nationals' ask one-half billion dollars apart over the five-year period? The parties spilled considerable ink editorializing about their apparently mutual dissatisfaction with the Agreement…. But while there can be no doubt those sentiments bear on the parties' calculations, the Agreement authorizes the RSDC only to apply its established methodology to assess the fair market value of the Nationals' rights for 2012-2016, not to enforce or tilt other contractual provisions in light of the parties' perceived slights. Looking ahead to the next Negotiation Period in 2016, the Nationals and Orioles would be better served finding more substantial common ground before invoking Section 2.J.3 [appeal to arbitration by the RSDC]. The Agreement, after all, describes MASN as a commercially cooperative venture."

8 - THE EIGHTH INNING – THE JUDGE TRIES TO FIGURE IT OUT

"In a court with one of the busiest dockets in the nation, Judge Berman was dazzled by the headlights of professional sports and crossed into the wrong lane and engaged the federal courts in the intricacies of running a sports league. Where they have no business." – former National Basketball Association Commissioner David Stern's reaction to the New York federal trial judge's ruling in favor of New England Patriots quarterback Tom Brady in the "Deflategate" cheating scandal - from "The Incredible Shrinking Commissioner" by S.L. Price in *Sports Illustrated* magazine, September 14, 2015

At the Hearing

Mr. Buckley (Nationals' lawyer):

"So the thesis of their entire case here, think about it for a minute, is that Mr. Manfred and others and MLB staff, who report to the Commissioner and then to the owners and whose employment is controlled by them, would subvert the entire RSDC process because one of the law firms that Baseball happens to hire is Proskauer, and Proskauer happens to represent the Nationals.

Now, that's crazy, I would submit...."

A Precedent or Only a Portent? The "Deflategate" Decision - For the Third Time, A Federal Trial Judge Overturns an NFL Commissioner's Arbitration Disciplinary Decision

In the so-called "Deflategate" scandal, the New England Patriots National Football League team was accused of doctoring the air pressure in footballs used in their 2015 conference championship game against the Indianapolis Colts. By reducing the air pressure in the footballs, team staff allegedly made them easier for quarterback Tom Brady to throw. An Indianapolis Colts player complained to a referee during the game that a thrown football was underinflated.

After the game ended with a Patriots victory, the National Football League (NFL) hired a law firm to help it to investigate whether the game footballs were underinflated, and whether they were intentionally underinflated by Patriots staff or players. The co-called "Wells Report", named for New York lawyer Ted Wells, concluded that

"It is more probable than not that New England Patriots personnel participated in violations of the Playing Rules and were involved in a deliberate effort to circumvent the rules."

The Wells Report identified two minor Patriots employees who allegedly "participated in a deliberate effort to release air from Patriots game balls after the balls were examined by the referee …" It concluded that "it is more probable than not that Brady was at least generally aware of the inappropriate activities of [Patriots employees] involving the release of air from Patriots game balls."

As punishment for these violations of "Playing Rules" that were provided to NFL owners by the league, the NFL Executive Vice President notified Tom Brady that he would be suspended from playing in the first four games of the 2015-2016 season. He also notified the Patriots' team owner that the owner would be fined $1 million, and that the team would forfeit its first round college draft choice in the 2016 NFL draft, and its fourth round choice in the 2017 NFL draft.

NFL Commissioner Roger Goodell, pursuant to the collective bargaining agreement with the players union, designated himself as the arbitrator to whom Tom Brady's appeal of this decision could be made. On appeal, Goodell confirmed the penalty imposed on Tom Brady. The Patriots' owner did not appeal the penalties imposed against himself or his team.

The NFL sued in the federal trial court for the Southern District of New York (next door to the New York County Supreme Court in Manhattan) to confirm Goodell's arbitration decision, anticipating that the players union would attempt to have it vacated by a judge. After two hearings in August 2015, federal Judge Richard Berman denied the NFL's motion to confirm the arbitrator's decision, and approved the union's motion to vacate it.

This was the third consecutive overturning of an NFL player suspension for violation of personal conduct policies. The indefinite suspension of Baltimore Ravens running-back Ray Rice for domestic violence was overturned in 2014 by a former federal trial judge appointed by the Commissioner to hear Rice's appeal. The suspension of Minnesota Vikings running-back Adrian Peterson for physical discipline of his child was overturned by a federal trial judge in 2015.

Judge Berman described his authority to vacate an arbitration award as "limited … but the deference due an arbitrator does not extend so far as to require a district court to countenance, much less confirm, an award obtained without the requisites of fairness or due process." Judge Berman interpreted the extent of the NFL Commissioner's authority as an arbitrator as limited by the "law of the shop", a kind of common law created by previous arbitration decisions under the authority of the collective bargaining agreement between the players union and the NFL.

He concluded that these previous decisions had recognized a right of disciplined players to "advance notice of prohibited conduct and potential discipline." In his opinion, Tom Brady had not received advance notice that he might be penalized with a four-game suspension for "general awareness of the inappropriate activities" of others, or for non-cooperation with the NFL's subsequent investigation of these activities.

Previous suspensions for the use of anabolic steroids were not comparable situations, despite the NFL's arguments to the contrary. Brady, according to the judge, had neither been notified of the wrongfulness of his alleged activities, nor of the possible punishment for them by game suspensions.

The overturning of the Ray Rice and Adrian Peterson arbitrator penalties were similar to the Tom Brady court decision in that they both involved a lack of advance notice of penalties. The

Rice and Peterson cases involved lack of advance notice of penalties that had been increased after the alleged domestic violence occurred.

Judge Berman concluded that the Brady suspension should be also be vacated, in addition to the lack of advance notice reason, because Commissioner Goodell improperly denied Brady the opportunity to examine NFL Executive Vice President Jeff Pash regarding his role as co-investigator of the ball deflation complaint. According to the judge, Goodell had denied Brady this opportunity by saying that Pash's testimony would be "cumulative", without further explanation. Judge Berman concluded that Brady was prejudiced by this lost chance to question his investigator.

Judge Berman also decided to vacate the arbitration decision because Brady had been improperly denied equal access to the NFL's investigative files, including interview notes. The NFL's investigators (and arbitration hearing counsel) did have access to those files.

Judge Berman noted that an arbitration award can be vacated for "evident partiality", but he explicitly did not address this claim as a basis for overturning the arbitration. His second and third reasons to vacate, because of the denial of a chance to interview the co-investigator, and the denial of equal access to the full investigative files, were not characterized by the judge as evidence of partiality by the arbitrator. They were, instead, additional evidence of the absence of fair procedures that would "give each of the parties to the dispute an adequate opportunity to present its evidence and argument."

Judge Berman's decision shows that a professional sports league arbitration can be vacated by a trial judge for unfair procedures. By avoiding Brady's claim of the Commissioner's "evident partiality" against him, however, this decision did not become a precedent for Peter Angelos's main argument to overturn MLB's arbitration award for the Nationals' cablecast rights fees.

The Orioles' First Argument at the Hearing - "… they were tainting and poisoning the arbitration …"

At the May 18, 2015 court hearing, Thomas Hall, attorney for MASN, the regional sports channel, argued that the arbitration decision of the RSDC should be vacated, because of the "evident partiality" of the arbitrators. Much of his argument concerned the multiple roles of the lawyers of the

Proskauer Rose law firm.

The Proskauer Rose law firm represented each of the MLB teams, of which the arbitrators were at least part-owners, on various legal matters, most of which related to MLB business. Hall argued that these representations increased after the dispute over the Nationals' rights fees began in 2012.

He argued that this multiple representation created an incentive for the lawyers to get even more work from the Rays, the Pirates and the Mets. He argued that it gave them an incentive to favor these owners and their teams, rather than the Orioles and its majority-owned regional sports channel, in determining the proper price for the Nationals' rights fees.

Mr. Hall (MASN lawyer):

"What should have happened in the first instance was, when we raised the issues with, 'the Nationals should gave gotten new counsel', they should have seen that they were tainting and poisoning the arbitration, subjecting it to later vacatur [the arbitration decision being vacated by a judge], and they should have voluntarily done something. Absent that, Major League Baseball should have taken action."

THE JUDGE TRIES TO FIGURE IT OUT

Judge Marks:

"Was it an appearance that it was poisoned or was it actually poisoned?

Mr. Hall:

"Well, we believe it was actually poisoned given the failure to apply established methodology ..."

Judge Marks:

"What did that have to do with Proskauer? That's a separate issue ..."

Mr. Hall:

"Well, the answer is: We don't know. We don't know what went on behind the scenes. We know that—

Judge Marks:

"Is this speculation then? What is the harm that was caused here? Can you articulate it?

Mr. Hall:

"Yes, your Honor. The harm is the taint, the suspicions, the lack of an unbiased, evidently impartial panel …"

Judge Marks:

"So it just looks bad or was it really bad because of Proskauer?"

Mr. Hall:

"We think it was really bad, your Honor, but your Honor need not reach that conclusion to vacate.

We have, your Honor, at the very same time, the inhouse lawyers for Major League Baseball are working on this arbitration, giving legal advice to the arbitrators, summarizing the submissions to the arbitrators, and sitting in with the arbitrators during their deliberations. These were inhouse lawyers in the Major League Baseball labor relations group. Proskauer was chief labor counsel to Major League Baseball at that time. These inhouse lawyers were working on this arbitration, must have been dealing with Proskauer daily in connection with Proskauer's representation of Major League Baseball. We have no idea what was said, we have no idea what information was exchanged, we just don't know. But it does look bad, your Honor. Absolutely."

Mr. Hall denied that the Orioles-owned MASN knew when it signed the television contract that MLB would be involved in the arbitration process to the extent that it would later become involved. He noted that Proskauer had also represented Commissioner Rob Manfred, and his predecessor Bud Selig, on separate legal matters, and that one of MLB's in-house lawyers who worked on the arbitration had previously worked for Proskauer.

The Orioles' Second Argument - "Evident partiality will be ... where a reasonable person would have to conclude that an arbitrator was partial to one party ..."

Thomas Hall criticized the arbitrators for their failure to voluntarily disclose to MASN their relationships with Proskauer, and for "a failure to investigate by the arbitrators as to what relationships they did have with Proskauer."

Hall argued that the standard for "evident partiality" that justified vacating an arbitration award was that "Evident partiality will be found where a reasonable person would have to conclude that an arbitrator was partial to one party to the arbitration." He argued that the arbitration decision should be vacated if either a member of the arbitration panel, or MLB itself, was evidently partial to one party.

Hall argued that the possibly relaxed judicial scrutiny of an internal industry arbitration should not be applied where a "totally unnecessary relationship" was created by the Proskauer firm also advising the Nationals as their counsel during the arbitration.

Hall admitted that Proskauer had also represented the Orioles in a legal matter when the rights fees arbitration began. The firm withdrew as the Orioles' counsel in that matter, however, when the Orioles complained that there was a conflict in their representation of both arbitration parties in different matters.

Hall argued that the Orioles did not waive their objections to the partiality of the Proskauer lawyer-advisors by continuing to participate in the arbitration after objecting. He alleged that MLB failed to disclose the full extent and range of legal matters on which Proskauer advised both MLB and its clubs, and that MLB denied access by the Orioles to the clubs to learn more about those matters.

The Judge Questions What Kind of Arbitration This Was - "So it was anticipated that this would be incestuous by nature; there would be intertwining relationships among the different parties and maybe law firms?"

Judge Marks questioned Orioles' lawyer Arnold Weiner about the Orioles' expectations for the type of arbitration that was required under the television contract.

Judge Marks:

"So was it anticipated that this would be incestuous by nature; there would be intertwining relationships among the different parties and maybe law firms? Is that something that could have been anticipated at the outset?"

Mr. Weiner:

"You could have anticipated at the outset that there would be people who were familiar with the matter, and that was necessary.

What you could not have anticipated ... was that ... we would come to an arbitration in which our adversary would be the one law firm that represented everybody else in the room except us at the time, and, in fact, had represented us but fired us....

And under Mr. Manfred's direction, from 2007 on, which was after our Settlement Agreement, the relationships between Proskauer and Major League Baseball simply skyrocketed....

Why are these relationships important? Why do they bear on this arbitration?.... It's because ... [t]hese relationships are relationships of trust and confidence. These are relationships in which the highest officials of Baseball trust their lawyers with their most important problems, they share their confidences with these very lawyers about their major problems, and they seek out the advice and counsel the word of these lawyers. These are the lawyers who Baseball and the arbitrators are used to listening to. They have instant credibility. Their word matters. It matters day in and day out."

Mr. Weiner emphasized the role played by former Proskauer lawyers in negotiating the collective bargaining agreement between MLB and the players union in 2011.

Mr. Weiner:

"The Major League Baseball Collective Bargaining Negotiations.... ended on December 23rd of 2011, which is about 12 or 15 days before our arbitration began. And this was a career-builder literally for Mr. Manfred and Mr. Halem. Their career was extraordinarily enhanced by being able to pull off this collective bargaining agreement, and throughout this entire time, they worked hand in glove with Mr. Laccese [chairman of the Proskauer law firm] to accomplish this, only to have Mr. Laccese show up two weeks later as the lawyer for the Nationals in our arbitration....

Then on January 27th, which is now three weeks into the arbitration and literally on the eve of the organizational meeting and prehearing conference where we were told that Proskauer would not be precluded from being in this case, Mr. Selig himself personally hires Proskauer to negotiate his five-year employment contract; a matter of great significance to him because it is a matter of – a large economic matter that was of extreme – had to be of great importance....

[F]our new [legal] matters ... are opened throughout May [2012]... and ... this extremely important matter for Baseball. It's the internal organization of Baseball, the Office of the Commissioner is being reorganized, and it's a huge matter. You can see that it went on from May 2nd of 2012, all the way until April of 2014 … and there were 49 different Proskauer timekeepers [lawyers charging by the hour] who were involved in that project….

Major League Baseball, MLB actually controlled … the procedures, the organizational meeting, the refusal to preclude Proskauer, and the grant of the continuing objection [by the Orioles to Proskauer's participation], and the information flow to the arbitrators….

Mr. Manfred and his staff participated in every deliberation [of the arbitrators] that we have been made aware of."

The New and Different Role of the Revenue Sharing Definitions Committee as Arbiter of a Two-Party Dispute

The MLB Revenue Sharing Definitions Committee handles many team television cost and revenue projections for the purpose of revenue sharing allocations. As the following dialogue indicates, however, these financial projections are a matter resolved solely between one club and MLB (acting for all the other clubs). Revenue sharing disputes are unlike the two-party adversarial arbitration of rights fees required by the 2005 MLB-Orioles television contract.

The different nature of these two types of RSDC proceedings caused the Orioles to raise the issue of whether the advisory role of MLB lawyers in a one-club proceeding might not be appropriate for a two-club proceeding. (MLB and Peter Angelos might have thought more deeply about this before they agreed to resolve rights fees disputes through RSDC arbitration.)

Judge Marks:

"Did we know, is there anything in the record, and we think this may have been the first arbitration that was conducted by this Committee, the Standing Committee, but in the other work that the Standing Committee does, does the Commissioner's office generally serve as this gatekeeping function? Do we know?

Mr. Weiner:

"I would assume so. We don't know for sure, but I would assume so. It's a one-party matter."

Judge Marks:

"Well, it's not an adversarial proceeding, so it's different. Okay."

The Orioles' Third Argument - The $25 Million Loan From MLB to The Nationals Gave MLB An Incentive to Increase the Arbitration Award

The Orioles' third argument to vacate the arbitration decision concerned a loan made from the Office of the Commissioner to the Nationals. It was intended to reduce the financial impact on the Nationals of the non-payment of cablecast rights fees during the course of the arbitration, and during MLB's subsequent negotiations to sell MASN to Comcast.

On August 26, 2013, MLB signed a Loan Agreement with the Nationals to lend the club $25 million, and according to Mr. Weiner "if there is … such an RSDC award, then that will be the source for the repayment to Major League Baseball." This produced the following dialogue about which club benefited from MLB's loan.

Judge Marks:

"Wasn't it clear that during this period there

were discussions about MASN being bought out by another company?....

In effect, wasn't that the purpose for the long delay in the publication of the arbitration award? ....

Wasn't that the major reason that there was an effort in the Commissioner's office that the Commissioner's office thought that the whole thing could be resolved?....

Didn't that favor, that delay, at least favor the Orioles as much as it favored the Nationals?"

Mr. Weiner:

"Oh, if it could be sold. Certainly. Certainly. But the payment wasn't in our interest....

If this was an aboveboard transaction, we would have been told about it, we would have been shown this Agreement, we would have – there would have been nothing to hide from us. This was all done behind our back. We never would have agreed to it."

The Orioles' Argument That a Vacated Award Should Not Be Returned to MLB for a Do-Over

The Orioles' third lawyer, Carter Phillips, then argued that, if the arbitration decision were to be vacated, it should not be returned to an MLB arbitration panel for a new decision, because of MLB's continuing financial interest in having its loan repaid from the arbitration award.

Mr. Phillips:

"Now, unless you're going to say that's a complete sham, which in context maybe it was, but it certainly then suggests precisely my last argument, which is why you cannot send this back to the Commissioner under the circumstances of this case. But I cannot imagine any circumstance in which you allow the ultimate decision-maker essentially to enter into an agreement whereby the amount of money turns completely on his final resolution of the case."

Phillips then argued that the arbitration panel used its "own brand of industrial justice" (the same phrase used by federal Judge Berman to overturn the Tom Brady four-game suspension by the NFL Commissioner) by departing from the assumption of a 20% profit margin for a regional sports network, such as MASN.

Mr. Phillips:

"The now-Commissioner himself, has recognized that if a regional sports network has ever achieved 20 percent, then they automatically get a presumptive 20 percent, and it can only go up, it never goes down in the circumstances that were applied in this case...."

Judge Marks:

"Is this different though? Could the argument be made that this is a different matter entirely?"

Mr. Phillips:

"And that is the argument they make, that this is different. But the problem with that is, that is precisely the decision to develop your own brand of industrial justice....

And what's clear as a bell in the arbitrators' own decision, the panel's decision, Footnote 2 specifically says: "Because we're not applying the methodology we apply to every other network, this is not going to be precedent for any other network.'...."

Judge Marks:

"Isn't the situation somewhat *sui generis* [one of a kind]?

First of all, is there another network that is owned by two separate teams?....

The Orioles' ownership share of the network is what percentage?"

Mr. Phillips:

"It was 90 percent at the time of the ... Agreement and it decreases by one percent every year ..."

Judge Marks:

"Is this an apples and oranges situation then?"

Mr. Phillips:

"No. It's apples and apples, in the sense that the deal that the parties struck, that Major League Baseball struck with the Orioles, was that: "We will guarantee you in determining the fair market value ... the fair market value will be the established methodology applied to every other network."

The Nationals First Argument – "A Showing of Evident Partiality Must Be Direct and Not Speculative"

Stephen Neuwirth, the first lawyer to argue for the Nationals, presented "at least three reasons why vacating the RSDC's award here and not confirming it would constitute blatant reversible error."

Mr. Neuwirth:

"The first reason is legal.... [T]he arbitration agreement must be governed by the standards under the Federal Arbitration Act ...

Now, here, the entire argument that has been made in favor of vacating the arbitration award is premised on there having been some appearance of bias in the arbitration proceeding ....

Now, the Federal Arbitration Act has a different standard....

Evident partiality will be found where a

reasonable person would have to conclude that an arbitrator was partial to one party to the arbitration. It is a stringent standard that could not be satisfied by a mere appearance of bias....

The problem is, there is no evidence that there was any undue influence on this process....

And ... the Second Circuit ... says: 'A showing of evident partiality must be direct and not speculative.'"

Judge Marks:

"Wouldn't that require circumstantial evidence that one [of] the arbitrators said 'I'm ruling for Proskauer's client because I trust Proskauer'?....

You would never have something like that."

Mr. Neuwirth:

"Well – but that's why the process is to defer to arbitrators....

For example, what we don't have in this case is any evidence that there was, in fact, one of these ex parte [outside of the knowledge of the other party] communications [between Proskauer and

an RSDC member or MLB] that the petitioners are saying naturally would have occurred....
So in the absence of that, there is – it's purely speculative to assert that the fact that these relationships existed at the time somehow means that there was an undue influence on the process, and we're going to see just the opposite occurred."

Judge Marks:

"Look, I can't believe the rule is that extreme. Obviously this wasn't the case here, but what if Proskauer was personally representing each of the arbitrators on this Committee, each of the three, while the arbitration was pending? You're saying that that wouldn't be enough?....

You know something, if that's the law, with all due respect, that doesn't make any sense. It really doesn't...."

Mr. Neuwirth:

"Well, at the very least, we don't have something that extreme here, as I think your Honor recognized."

Judge Marks:

"I agree with that."

The Nationals' Second Argument – A Court May Not Correct An Arbitrator's Mistakes in Applying the Rights Fees Valuation Methodology

Mr. Neuwirth then addressed the issue of the RSDC allegedly not following the established methodology for determining the fair market value of a regional sports channel.

Mr. Neuwirth:

"But it's indisputable that the RSDC did what the contract said it should do. And in New York, even if there is an argument that the arbitrators made a blatant error in the way that they interpreted the contract, it's not the place of a court to go back and try to redo what the arbitrators did."

Mr. Neuwirth argued that the Orioles and MASN were using their appeal of the arbitration decision as a delaying tactic to force the Nationals into the position of accepting inadequate rights fees in order to avoid an even longer squeeze on their budget.

Judge Marks then questioned the meaning of the "established methodology" to be applied by the arbitrators.

Judge Marks:

"Well, if they have incorrectly applied the methodology, applied the wrong methodology, would I be able to second-guess that?"

Mr. Neuwirth:

"If all it says is 'apply the established methodology,' and the arbitrators undertake to apply the established methodology, even if you think they were completely wrong in how they did that, you cannot reverse them. You cannot vacate the award. And the case law, which we will look at, says that....

[I]f, in fact, the Orioles believed that this contract, if they really thought this meant that they were guaranteed 20 percent, they never told that to the Executive Council of Major League Baseball when it voted to approve the transaction, voted to approve the Agreement....

[T]he U.S. Supreme Court in Oxford Health Plans versus Sutter, decided in 2013, ... says: '...

convincing a court of an arbitrator's error – even his grave error – is not enough. So long as the arbitrator was 'arguably construing' the contract – which this one was – a court may not correct his mistakes.... The potential for those mistakes is the price of agreeing to arbitration .... the courts have no business overruling him because their interpretation of the contract is different from his. The arbitrator's construction holds, however good, bad or ugly.'"

Mr. Phillips then cited Peter Angelos's testimony before the Congress on April 7, 2006 that

" 'The ultimate control as to what is going to be paid for the rights from period to period is in the hands of Major League Baseball and will remain there. If at any time the Nationals would be dissatisfied with the fee structure, the rights fee structure, they have a right to complain to Major League Baseball and demand not that Bortz be applied, demand that a survey be made to guarantee that fair market value payments are being made for the rights fee for the rights to their games.'"

Mr. Phillips continued.

"Now, if that isn't clear enough to expose the

duplicity of what is happening in this process .... it is just a fact that the information that has been presented to your Honor about this process by MASN and the Orioles is, we would respectfully submit, false and in some cases misleading."

The Nationals' Third Argument – If Any Party Improperly Influenced the Arbitrators, It Was the Orioles' Lawyer, Not the Nationals' Lawyers

Mr. Neuwirth then addressed the argument of evident partiality/bias created by the participation of current and former Proskauer lawyers in the arbitration.

Mr. Neuwirth:

"This whole argument about Proskauer completely overlooks, as your Honor correctly noted this morning, that this is supposed to be an inside baseball arbitration in front of the RSDC.... So putting aside anything having to do with counsel, we are starting out with very close relationships between the parties and the arbitrators....

And, again, the suggestion that a law firm could

have an influence that would trump those relationships among the owners, we think is farfetched and, in fact, the only evidence shows the opposite."

Neuwirth then argued that the only evidence of efforts to improperly influence the arbitrators was related to actions by the Orioles, who participated in the arbitration despite the Nationals' objection that MASN and the Nationals should have been the only parties to the arbitration.

Mr. Neuwirth:

"Who did the Orioles show up with as their counsel? Alan Rifkin.... Mr. Rifkin is not just some ordinary counsel. Mr. Rifkin is known by everyone not only to be Mr. Angelos's right-hand man in the running of his team, but someone who regularly appears for him at owners' meetings, effectively as his alter ego....

This is supposed to be an inside baseball arbitration. The Orioles knew that. That's why they showed up with Mr. Rifkin. The suggestion that Proskauer was going to have more influence on these arbitrators than Mr. Rifkin is fantasy .... Proskauer was the hired help. Mr. Rifkin was upstairs with the owners. Proskauer was downstairs with the hired help."

Judge Marks:

"Why wasn't the extent of the Proskauer representation disclosed?"

Mr. Neuwirth:

"Well, I would answer it this way.... How is it that at the start of this lawsuit, when the Orioles came with MASN to complain to your Honor about all of the Proskauer relationships, they were able to tell your Honor about so much more than appeared in these disclosures? The reason is because they did a public record search and pulled up what they could...."

Judge Marks:

"Wasn't there a duty on Major League Baseball to investigate and disclose?"

Mr. Neuwirth:

"The court said, this is a 2007 case, '...courts have declined to vacate awards because of undisclosed relationships where the complaining party should have known of the relationship or could have learned of it before or during the arbitration, rather than after it lost.' "

Neuwirth then continued with his argument that it was the Orioles, rather than the Nationals or MLB, who were trying to improperly influence the arbitrators.

Mr. Neuwirth:

"And they didn't only bring Mr. Rifkin, they brought the head of Bortz. The suggestion that the head of Bortz [Mr. Wyche], who works regularly with the RSDC, wasn't going to influence the RSDC, is also not believable.... They did exactly what they are accusing the Nationals of doing. They brought people that they knew could influence this process. And certainly there is every reason to believe that Mr. Rifkin had more of an influence than Proskauer did. In fact, that is what the evidence shows....

The key here is, there's no evidence that Proskauer had any ex parte communication with anyone. No evidence. But there is lots of evidence of ex parte communications by Mr. Rifkin."

Neuwirth cited, as evidence of this, a statement

THE JUDGE TRIES TO FIGURE IT OUT

by Commissioner Manfred that

" 'Mr. Rifkin ... repeatedly initiated conversations with me about the merits of the RSDC Proceeding where no representative of the Nationals was present. Mr. Rifkin's unilateral communications frequently involved his advocacy on behalf of MASN and the Orioles ... and ... [t]he fair market value of the Nationals' telecast rights for 2012 through 2016. Some of these unilateral communications took place before the merits hearing and shortly after the merits hearing, before the RSDC had finished deliberating.' "

Neuwirth argued that the *ex parte* communications by the Orioles' lawyer were motivated by a desire to improve the return from a possible sale of MASN.

Mr. Neuwirth:

"But what we know from the documents that have now been produced is that what Mr. Rifkin was doing behind the scenes was working to prevent this award from ever being released to try to pressure the Nationals to make a deal....

It is remarkable – remarkable -- that MASN and

the Orioles have had the gumption to tell your Honor what they have said about this $25 million payment.

In this e-mail to Mr. Rifkin, Mr. Manfred says: '... we have invested $25 million to buy time.' Just as your Honor noted. There was no trick here. This was done because the Orioles were trying to pressure the Nationals to make a deal that the Orioles wanted that was going to let them get a billion dollars of value out of MASN ....

Mr. Manfred described the terms that MLB and Mr. Rifkin were discussing, which include.... 'We understand that the agreement [to sell MASN] would have to eliminate any possibility of issuing the current RSDC opinion.' In other words, the Nationals were not going to get what they were entitled to."

The Nationals' Fourth Argument – The Orioles Franchise Value Has Already Increased by the Amount Represented by the Rights Fees They Are Disputing

Finally, Neuwirth argued that the Orioles' franchise value had already increased by an amount that assumed the payment of rights fees at least as large as those determined by the arbitrators.

Mr. Neuwirth:

"Bloomberg in 2013 valued the Orioles at $1.12 billion when factoring in the team's majority stake in regional sports network MASN. That amount, in fact, is very consistent with the projections of rights fees that the Nationals made, and it is completely inconsistent with what were truly the lowball numbers that MASN and the Orioles put forth.

And why is MASN pushing – why are the Orioles pushing so hard on the Nationals to make a deal? Because they want to cash out that value and force the Nationals, who are strapped for cash, to participate in that because they won't have any other way to get the cash...."

The Nationals' Fifth Argument – There Was No Conflict of Interest in Proskauer Rose Lawyers Representing the Nationals, MLB and the Arbitrators' Clubs, and the Orioles Knew It

John Buckley addressed the argument that MLB hid the extent of Proskauer's legal representation of MLB from the Orioles.

Mr. Buckley:

"Major League Baseball was never asked by MASN or the Orioles for a list of each and every representation undertaken in the past or during the RSDC proceeding. So it responded open-endedly that: Yes, we used Proskauer for these and other matters, but there was no demand for a specification of each and every matter.

What we know is MASN and the Orioles knew about those other representations....

And there was no objection to Mr. Manfred, to the Major League Baseball staff, playing its historic supporting role....

So, knowing all that, and not objecting to participation of the Major League Baseball staff in a support role, how can they come into court today and complain that somehow that relationship tainted the process, when we know that —"

Judge Marks:

"Didn't they really learn, the further detail of the Commissioner's office's involvement in the arbitration proceeding, didn't they learn that subsequent to commencing this lawsuit?"

Mr. Buckley:

"Yes, but did it materially add to what they already knew? If they knew –"

Judge Marks:

"That's the question."

Mr. Buckley :

"-- they haven't shown it, even argued it....

I mean, if the relationship was objectionable; that is, if the fact that the staff was interacting with Proskauer in these other unrelated matters – as to which there was no conflict of interest by the way, no conflict of interest – if they already knew that, what does it matter that there were five or ten more matters or 20 more matters, if the fundamental problem is the very existence of the attorney-client relationship which already existed....

If it's an unrelated representation and there's no conflict of interest, then there's no partiality evident or non evident....

In all these cases ... all of the owners and clubs were in the same boat. Their interests are all aligned....

You talk about cases where arbitrators are challenged, is because of conflicts of interest, not because of unrelated representations in which the interests are aligned. That seems to have gotten lost in the whole discussion today."

Mr. Buckley continued his argument that the MLB staff is neutral in its dealings with different clubs.

Mr. Buckley:

"The staff is involved quite frequently in helping the Commissioner resolve disputes between and among the clubs, if the clubs have issues that need to be resolved. In that process, the staff has to be strictly neutral. They can't favor one club over the other. So that's in their DNA. It's what they do every day, is deal with disputes between the clubs and be neutral in those matters. They can't favor one club over the other.

So the thesis of their entire case here, think about it for a minute, is that Mr. Manfred and others and MLB staff, who report to the Commissioner and then to the owners and whose employment is controlled by them, would subvert the entire RSDC process because one of the law firms that Baseball happens to hire is Proskauer, and Proskauer happens to represent the Nationals.

Now, that's crazy, I would submit...."

Judge Marks:

"Although, I don't know, if I were the owner of the Nationals involved in this dispute, I could see why I would want to retain Proskauer to represent me in this proceeding. There might be a perception that they would have more influence over the outcome than some other law firm might have because they are so immersed in kind of what goes on in the day-to-day operations of Baseball. So it's not a completely farfetched premise."

Mr. Buckley:

"Let's take that – two different answers to that.

The first response is that we know that Proskauer were legal advisors to the Lerner family going back to the period even before they owned the club.... So they weren't brought in at the last minute to say: 'Oh, we get a leg up, here's Proskauer.'....

Second, who were the decision-makers? Rob Manfred wasn't going to dictate the issue. It was the three members of the RSDC ... who had at the time no relationship at all with Proskauer....

They [the Orioles] wanted Proskauer to be disqualified from representing the Nationals before the RSDC, and that was because of Proskauer's work for Major League Baseball. That was the request. They never asked for or objected to the removal of any other members of the RSDC.... Mr. Manfred advised them, as a matter of law, advised MASN and the Orioles that the RSDC is an arbitration tribunal, had no authority under the law to disqualify counsel.... and they said: 'All right, we still object but we're going to go ahead.' That's what happened."

The Nationals' Sixth Argument – The Arbitration Panel Had No Duty to Investigate the Extent of Proskauer Lawyers' Representation of the Arbitrators, Absent Evidence of Conflict of Interest

Judge Marks and Mr. Buckley then returned to the issue of whether the RSDC panel had a duty to disclose fully or to investigate any conflict of interest by the Proskauer lawyers representing MLB and the clubs.

Mr. Buckley:

"The [Applied Industries case] court said: 'There is no freestanding duty to investigate or disclose if you are an arbitrator under the FAA.' What is your duty[?] Your duty is to disclose, if you know – it's a knowledge requirement – or have reason to know of a nontrivial conflict of interest…."

Judge Marks:

"If you are asked to disclose, do you have to investigate?"

Mr. Buckley:

"No. If you know about, if you know about a nontrivial conflict of interest, that triggers the duty to investigate. But, again, there has to be knowledge, reason, and there has to be a conflict of interest. And in all of the litigations, if I had a drum to beat on, this is the drum I would beat on, you have to focus on conflict of interest. It's a clear line where basically in all these cases where Major League Baseball is hiring outside counsel to represent it, Proskauer, whoever, the interests of the clubs are aligned. There is no conflict. They are all in the same boat. Whether it's wage and hours case, whether it's antitrust challenge, whether it's the umpires suing, or somebody else, they're suing the institution of baseball. There are 30 clubs, 30 owners. There is no conflict of interest."

The Nationals Seventh Argument - The $25 Million Loan From MLB to the Nationals Was Good For the Orioles

Next, Buckley addressed the $25 million loan by MLB to the Nationals.

Mr. Buckley:

"Let me talk about the loan because there has been talk about it being a loan or an advance being a stake in the outcome....

By August, 2013, it's been two years into the new term of the contract, and the Nationals have had no economic relief even though everyone knows what the award is going to be.

The Nationals were pressing for issuance of the award immediately....

On the other hand, the Orioles were very interested in MASN, or in the sale to Comcast for a billion dollars, and they wanted discussions to continue. That was the dilemma. So what the Commissioner decided to do, Commissioner Selig, was, in the interests of both parties,.... [H]e said: '.... We're going to give an advance to the Nationals, representing the difference or delta between what MASN was paying and what the RSDC provision provided.' So what Major League Baseball was doing was stepping into the shoes of MASN and making a payment on MASN's behalf. It wasn't a gift, it was advance. And there was no stake in the outcome. The outcome was known.... Major League Baseball would reimburse in one of two ways; either, one, the award would eventually issue, and the funds that MASN would have to pay to the Nationals, a portion of that was sent to Major League

Baseball; or two, it would be a sale transaction to Comcast, in which case Major League Baseball would be paid out of the proceeds of that sale."

The Nationals' Eighth Argument - Preventing MLB From Rehearing Any Overturned Arbitration Award Would Create Further Payment Delay

Next, Buckley argued against the Orioles' demand that, if the arbitration award were vacated, the rights fees decision should be sent to some arbitrators other than the RSDC.

Mr. Buckley:

"So, there's no basis to remand to a different forum. You can't rewrite the contract. The contract says the RSDC. That's what the parties chose.

The composition of the RSDC has all been – two of the three members have changed....

So we're two years away from the next RSDC proceeding.

If grounds ... suffice to overturn the award ...

consider the practical consequences of these parties that are locked into this open-ended contract with no termination date, every five years, another RSDC proceeding. This is a train crash that's already happened and about to happen again; all the more reason not to disturb an award when there is no indication that any of the arbitrators were biased or impartial to either side, where they had no ex parte communications, and there was no conflict of interest in any of the representations."

The Nationals' Ninth Argument – There Was No Manifest Disregard of the Law By The Arbitrators

Finally, Mr. Buckley addressed the Orioles' claim that the arbitrators ignored the terms of the contract in making their award.

Mr. Buckley:

"With regard to manifest disregard of the law, as your Honor knows, that's a doctrine of last resort, rarely applied, and particularly in the context of contracts. As long as … the tribunal gave a barely colorable justification, then courts will not disturb arbitrators' interpretations of contracts, even if wrong.…

The only reason to go to arbitration is for cost and efficiency and finality; finality meaning that once the award is issued, that's the decision, and you can't call that into question based on legal or factual error in the award, with no recourse to the courts."

The Orioles Argument Against The Alleged Improper Influence Attempt By Their Lawyer – Separate Party Communications With MLB Was the Established Procedure

Mr. Weiner, for the Orioles, countered the Nationals' argument that the Orioles' lawyer, Mr. Rifkin, had made *ex parte* (outside of the knowledge of the other party) communications with Rob Manfred to try to influence MLB to favor the Orioles.

Mr. Weiner:

"These were not ex parte communications. Mr. Manfred set up a procedure. The procedure in his method of operation was to talk to each side separately....

After the arbitration began, and there had actually been this organizational meeting, he separately talked to the two sides about disqualifying Proskauer....

In fact, Mr. Manfred has e-mails in which he says: 'I'll talk to you Mr. Rifkin, but – and I'm going to meet with you, I need to meet with the Nationals first.'"

With that final argument by the Orioles' lawyers, the hearing ended at 1:30 p.m. on May 18, 2015.

Judge Marks Decides The Case

On November 4, 2015, Judge Lawrence Marks issued his decision. He first set the parameters for his ability to vacate the arbitration award by noting that a petition to vacate an arbitration award was

"a not uncommon application to a court yet one that is rarely granted....

Judicial review of arbitration awards is extremely limited.... the party seeking to vacate the award has the burden of proof.... The showing required to avoid confirmation [of the award] is 'very high'."

Judge Marks then addressed each of the Orioles' arguments in relation to the requirements for vacating an award set forth in the Federal Arbitration Act (FAA). Judge Marks noted that the FAA rules applied to the arbitration because

> "Where a contract containing an arbitration provision 'affects' interstate commerce, disputes arising thereunder are subject to the FAA."

Award Procured Through Corruption, Fraud, or Undue Means

Judge Marks noted that "the evidence must be 'abundantly clear' " that the award was procured through corruption, fraud or undue means in order for it to be vacated. He stated, regarding the allegedly corrupt means used to ensure an award favoring the Nationals, that

> "While MASN and the Orioles have established that they are disappointed in the RSDC Award, they have not provided 'abundantly clear' evidence of the alleged fraud or conspiracy."

The Nationals and MLB were 1-for-1 in their arguments.

Award Exceeding the Arbitrator's Scope of Authority, or Made With Manifest Disregard of the Law

Echoing federal Judge Berman's analysis, in vacating NFL Commissioner Roger Goodell's four-game suspension of New England Patriots quarterback Tom Brady, Judge Marks noted

" 'It is only when an arbitrator strays from the interpretation and application of the agreement and effectively dispenses his or her own brand of justice...that an arbitration decision may be vacated on this ground.... So the sole question ... is whether the arbitrator (even arguably) interpreted the parties' contract, not whether he got its meaning right or wrong.' "

Regarding "manifest disregard of the law", he noted that this "is a 'severely limited' doctrine.... of last resort limited to the rare occurrences of apparent 'egregious impropriety' on the part of the arbitrators ..." It required a judge to find

"... 'both that (1) the arbitrators knew of a governing legal principle yet refused to apply it or ignored it altogether, and (2) the law ignored by the arbitrators was well defined, explicit, and clearly applicable to the case.' "

Judge Marks stated that the claim of MASN, and of the Orioles, that the RSDC was required to apply a rights fees valuation methodology that would provide MASN with at least a 20% operating margin was not supported by any "well defined, explicit and clearly applicable" authority, particularly in the agreement itself.

"The arbitrators, by contrast, set forth an extensive explanation of their determination of the appropriate methodology to apply…. Their explanation, reasonable on its face, is more than sufficient to offer 'a barely colorable justification for the outcome' under the FAA, and therefore must be upheld even if this Court were to conclude that the RSDC's interpretation of its own established methodology was legally and factually incorrect."

The Nationals and MLB were 2-for-2 in their arguments.

Prejudicial Misconduct by the Arbitrators

Judge Marks noted that the FAA allows the vacating of an award

" '… where the arbitrators were guilty of

misconduct in refusing to postpone the hearing, upon sufficient cause shown, or in refusing to hear evidence pertinent and material to the controversy; or of any other misbehavior by which the rights of any party have been prejudiced....[M]isconduct occurs under this provision only where there is a denial of fundamental fairness.'"

Judge Marks rejected the MASN/Orioles argument that MLB "improperly controlled or influenced the arbitration process ..." He stated that

"With regard to misconduct solely as to process, very little was establish [sic] by those seeking to vacate the award, who have the burden of proof."

MASN and the Orioles, he noted, should have expected the MLB staff to help the arbitrators with certain tasks, and that the arbitrators would accept that help "to the extent customary and appropriate." It was "generally akin to the support that a law clerk provides to a judge, or that the staff of an established arbitration organization may provide to its arbitral panels."

The Nationals and MLB were 3-for-3 in their

arguments.

"Evident Partiality" Against MASN and the Orioles from MLB's $25 Million Loan to the Nationals

Judge Marks noted that

"The FAA provides that an arbitration award may be vacated 'where there was evident partiality or corruption in the arbitrators'....

[The New York test for this is whether] a reasonable person would have to conclude that an arbitrator was partial to one party to the arbitration....[and it] could not be satisfied by a mere appearance of bias ..."

Regarding MLB's $25 million loan to the Nationals, Judge Marks stated that

"MASN and the Orioles have not established that MLB's $25 million loan or advance to the Nationals, repayable from the proceeds of the RSDC Award, gives MLB or its standing committee an impermissible interest in the award under the specific circumstances presented."

The amount of the award did not change during MLB's unsuccessful negotiations to sell MASN to Comcast from 2012 until 2014. Therefore, Judge Marks stated that

> "Under these circumstances, the Court cannot see how MASN or the Orioles were actually prejudiced by MLB's financial arrangement with the Nationals, even assuming there was insufficient disclosure of the precise nature of the arrangement."

Judge Marks stated that "there is no reason to suppose that the award would be reduced to the point that the Nationals would be unable to repay MLB $25 million from the total amounts due to it over a five-year period." Finally,

> "The advance was not undertaken in secret, and MASN and the Orioles have not demonstrated that the circumstances of the advance raise any serious questions about the fairness of the arbitration process."

The Nationals and MLB were 4-for-4 in their arguments.

"Evident Partiality" From Proskauer's Participation in the Arbitration

MASN, and the Orioles, argued that Proskauer's concurrent representation of the Nationals, MLB and the individual arbitrators, or their interests, showed evident partiality, and that it was exacerbated by MLB's failure to investigate or to disclose the full extent of such representations. These concurrent representations occurred from the beginning of the arbitration in 2012 through the issuance of the final award in 2014.

Thirty of these matters involved the Nationals or MLB. Three additional matters involved the arbitrators, or their interests. Four specific Proskauer attorneys (out of a firm of 700 lawyers) represented the Nationals in the arbitration, and also represented MLB in 27 matters during the arbitration.

Judge Marks stated that

"MASN, and the Orioles as its majority owner, clearly agreed to an 'inside baseball' arbitration, where the parties and arbitrators would all be industry insiders who knew each other and inevitably had many connections. What they did not agree to, however, was a situation in which

MASN's arbitration opponent, the Nationals, was represented in the arbitration by the same law firm that was concurrently representing MLB and one or more of the arbitrators and/or the arbitrators' clubs in other matters....

Accordingly, the key question here is whether Proskauer's various simultaneous but unrelated representations of virtually every participant in the arbitration *except for* MASN and the Orioles created a situation in which a reasonable person would have to conclude that the arbitrators were partial to the Nationals."

Judge Marks stated that "If 'appearance of bias' were the standard, this Court would have no hesitation in vacating the award." He noted, however, that this was not the applicable standard under the FAA.

Judge Marks remarked that, under the applicable FAA standard of "a reasonable person conclusion of evident partiality", it might have been "a simple decision ... to confirm the award if MLB, as administrator of the arbitration, had taken MASN's objections seriously, and actually done something about it." Among these possible actions, Judge Marks noted that

"Common-sense approaches might well have included one or more of the following: (a) encouraging the Nationals to retain other counsel, (b) instructing Proskauer to make sure that the specific attorneys who were representing the Nationals in this arbitration were completely screened from any and all legal representations of MLB, the arbitrators and/or the arbitrators' clubs, from the time the arbitration was initiated until the time the award was issued, (c) fully advising the arbitrators of MASN's concerns and directing them to investigate and fully disclose their and their clubs' current relationships with Proskauer, or even (d) keeping the parties advised of MLB's own various continuing – and increasing – retention of Proskauer during the relevant period…. Yet MLB did nothing, except assure [MASN and the Orioles] repeatedly that their concerns would be preserved and not waived by their participation before the RSDC."

After failing to find any previous cases vacating an arbitration award under similar circumstances, Judge Marks noted that

"An important policy reason for requiring full

disclosure of possible conflicts in arbitration is that the parties, rather than the courts, can decide how best to address them in the first instance.... But this purpose is surely thwarted in the extraordinarily rare case, such as this one, where a party's repeatedly asserted concerns about fairness, based on the information available to it, are simply ignored and dismissed with repeated assurances that such objections will not be waived by participation in the arbitration."

Judge Marks noted that

" '...proof of actual bias is not required. Rather, partiality can be inferred from objective facts inconsistent with impartiality.'....

Here, there are objective facts that are unquestionably inconsistent with impartiality. Had MLB, the arbitrators, the Nationals and/or Proskauer taken some reasonable step to address [MASN's and the Orioles'] concerns about the Nationals' choice of counsel in the arbitration – or indeed *any step at all* – the Court might well have been compelled to uphold the arbitral award under the FAA. But MASN and the Orioles have established that their well-documented concerns fell on entirely deaf ears.

Under the circumstances, the Court concludes that this complete inaction objectively demonstrates an utter lack of concern for fairness of the proceeding that is 'so inconsistent with basic principles of justice' that the award must be vacated....

Trust in the neutrality of the adjudicative process is the very bedrock of the FAA. It is upon that foundation, and in great reliance upon it, that courts can defer to processes decided upon and designed by private contract. But without neutrality, where partiality runs without even the semblance of a check, the alternative process created does not warrant – and cannot be given – the great deference that arbitrators, and their awards, are bestowed by courts under the FAA.

Accordingly, the RSDC Award is hereby vacated."

With that conclusion, Judge Marks returned the arbitration to MLB's RSDC Committee. He rejected the Orioles' argument that returning the arbitration to the RSDC would be futile, stating

"The Court, however, notes that re-writing the parties' Agreement is outside of its authority.

The Court emphasizes that because it is ultimately the Nationals' choice of counsel that created the conflict, the parties may wish to meet and confer as to whether the Nationals are willing and able to retain counsel who do not concurrently represent MLB or the individual arbitrators and their clubs, and thereby return to arbitration by the RSDC, however currently constituted, pursuant to the parties' Agreement. If the current conflict remains, the parties might meet and confer regarding whether they can agree to a different neutral dispute resolution process, such as [arbitration] 'before a three-person panel…of the American Arbitration Association…' "

9 - THE NINTH INNING – CONTRACTS, COMPETITION AND THE LESSONS OF BASEBALL

"The life of the law has not been logic: it has been experience. The felt necessities of the time, the prevalent moral and political theories, intuitions of public policy, avowed or unconscious, even the prejudices which judges share with their fellow-men, have had a good deal more to do than the syllogism in determining the rules by which men should be governed." – from *The Common Law* by Oliver Wendell Holmes, Jr.

"syllogism 1. (logic). An inference in which one proposition (the conclusion) follows necessarily from two other propositions, known as the premises." – *Wiktionary.org*

"People often make mistakes when reasoning syllogistically. For instance, from the premises some A are B, some B are C, people tend to come to a definitive conclusion that therefore some A are C. However, this does not follow according to the rules of classical logic.... Determining the validity of a syllogism involves determining whether all ... are accounted for." – *Wikipedia.org*

At the Hearing

Mr. Buckley (Nationals' lawyer):

"If grounds ... suffice to overturn the award ... consider the practical consequences of these parties that are locked into this open-ended contract with no termination date, every five years, another RSDC proceeding. This is a train crash that's already happened and about to happen again; all the more reason not to disturb an award when there is no indication that any of the arbitrators were biased or impartial to either side, where they had no ex parte communications, and there was no conflict of interest in any of the representations."

On November 4, 2015, by the decision and order of Judge Lawrence Marks, Jr. of the State Supreme Court for New York County, the 2014 decision of the MLB arbitration panel, awarding the Washington Nationals $298,128,078 for the rights to regionally cablecast their baseball games for the five seasons from 2012 to 2016, was vacated.

First, how will this decision affect how the Nationals, the Orioles, and Major League Baseball conduct their business? Second, what, if anything, does this decision, and the process that led to it, imply for American employees, who are increasingly bound by non-compete agreements? Third, what does this decision imply, for American business owners, employees and consumers, who are increasingly bound by mandatory arbitration clauses in their contracts?

How Will the Court Decision Affect the Washington Nationals Club and Its Owners?

The MLB arbitration award was vacated (overturned) by Judge Marks only because he concluded that the Proskauer Rose law firm's participation in the arbitration process was unfair to MASN and the Orioles. The Proskauer Rose lawyers represented the Nationals in the arbitration, and also advised, in one or more legal matters, MLB and the three club owners on the arbitration panel. They represented every party involved in the arbitration *except* the Orioles, and their majority-owned regional cable sports channel.

Judge Marks suggested that, for a re-arbitration of their dispute before an MLB panel, the Nationals should consider retaining lawyers "who do not concurrently represent MLB or the individual arbitrators and their clubs ..." Alternatively, if the Nationals are unwilling to find other lawyers to represent them, the next arbitration, he suggested, could be conducted before a "different, neutral" dispute resolution body, such as the American Arbitration Association (assuming that the apparently ubiquitous Proskauer Rose law firm does not also represent them).

Almost three-and-one-half years were consumed by the process of MLB arbitration, MLB-Comcast negotiations delay, and litigation in the New York state court. Theodore Lerner's Washington Nationals' club now faces another delay before another MLB arbitration panel will be able to make another award of cablecast rights fees for the 2012-2016 period.

This next MLB arbitration award will likely be for the same amount as the award made in 2012 by the previous MLB panel. Judge Marks stated in his decision that the methodology used by the MLB arbitration panel in 2012 was not a reason to overturn its award. So why would the next MLB arbitration panel change its methodology?

By the time that the next MLB panel makes its 2012-2016 period rights fees award, the Orioles and the Nationals will be required, by their 2005 Television Contract, to attempt to negotiate the regional cablecast rights fees for the Nationals' games for the baseball seasons from 2017 to 2021.

Is there any reason to expect that those negotiations will proceed more smoothly than the 2012 negotiations?

The inventiveness of well-funded, and indefatigable legal minds, like those of Peter Angelos and his legal team, should not be underestimated. More time will pass before a judge concludes that the Orioles have run out of avenues of appeal for an arbitration award that they agreed to accept without appeal in their 2005 contract.

The Orioles and the Nationals Seek Conflicting Orders from Judge Marks After His Decision to Vacate the MLB Arbitration

On December 11, 2015, the Orioles' legal team sprang into action to file an appeal of Judge Marks's overturning of the MLB arbitration award. *They appealed a decision that they won.* Why?

Probably because the Orioles' lawyers also saw a short road ahead from Judge Marks's decision to another MLB arbitration panel decision awarding the same amount in rights fees to the Nationals that was awarded by the 2012 panel. If the Nationals are represented in the next arbitration by lawyers who do not advise any other party involved in the arbitration, there will likely be no argument for the

Orioles to make on appeal of the next arbitration award that Judge Marks has not already rejected.

Were there any new arguments that the Orioles made in their December 2015 notice of appeal? The Orioles argued that

> "The Supreme Court's ruling that it lacked this authority as a matter of law [to order a rehearing before different arbitrators] was simply erroneous....
>
> As the prior proceedings demonstrate, MLB and the RSDC would be hopelessly and irreparably conflicted in any new RSDC arbitration."

The Orioles' appeal argument then repeated, in different language, the same allegations of "evident bias" that Judge Marks had rejected in his November, 2015 decision. Regarding the likely change in the club owner membership of the next RSDC arbitration panel, the argument continued that, because of the history of the litigation, and of statements by MLB Commissioner Robert Manfred supporting the previous arbitration award

> "No potential RSDC member can be neutral and impartial: the RSDC as a forum is conflicted and thoroughly compromised."

The Orioles' argument concluded with a statement that they had previously filed an arbitration petition with the American Arbitration Association claiming that MLB and the Nationals had breached the 2005 Television Contract. The matter was suspended pending the New York litigation.

On January 21, 2016, the Nationals' lawyers filed their motion with Judge Marks for an order by him to compel MASN and the Orioles to comply with his previous order by returning to the MLB Revenue Sharing Definitions Committee to arbitrate the rights fees dispute. Stephen Neuwirth, one of the Nationals' lawyers at the firm Quinn, Emanuel, Urquhart & Sullivan, which agreed to be their new MLB arbitration lawyers, submitted a copy of a letter from the Nationals to MASN and the Orioles showing that

> "Submitting to the Court's ruling, the Nationals informed MASN and [the Orioles], by letter dated November 25, 2015, that the Nationals would forego representation by the Proskauer firm, and would retain new counsel that does not concurrently represent MLB or the individual arbitrators or their clubs...."

Unfortunately, notwithstanding this significant act by the Nationals to choose new arbitration counsel, MASN and [the Orioles] have repeatedly refused the Nationals' requests to return to the RSDC for a new arbitration, instead insisting that any new arbitration must take place before a panel other than the RSDC .... MASN and the Orioles thus are purporting to grant themselves the non-RSDC arbitration forum that this Court declined to Order based on the parties' 2005 Telecast Agreement....

MASN and the Orioles are thus abusing the Court's ruling to foreclose the Nationals' bargained-for contractual right to an arbitration before the RSDC....

Further delay at this point in resolving the rights fees dispute for 2012-2016 would severely prejudice the Nationals.... Since 2012, MASN has unilaterally determined to pay the Nationals only rights fees based on the rejected formula that MASN and the Orioles had proposed during the original RSDC arbitration."

The Nationals' new lawyers argued that all requirements for an order compelling an MLB arbitration had been satisfied. First, the Nationals had selected new arbitration counsel that does not concurrently represent MLB or the members of the RSDC panel or their clubs.

Second, they argued that, under the Federal Arbitration Act, where the terms of an agreement to arbitrate are unambiguous, if one party refuses to arbitrate, a court should order them to arbitrate according to those terms.

Third, they argued that, the Nationals would be prejudiced by any continued delay in MLB arbitration, because they would continue to receive only below-market-value cablecast rights fees from MASN, contrary to the terms of the 2005 agreement. Examples of the effects of such inadequate fees were offered, including

"Without this added income, the Nationals are handicapped in their ability to invest in efforts to improve the team. For instance, ... the Nationals cannot bring full economic confidence to investments in multi-year player contracts to keep up with the fierce competition for top players especially when such control over finances is in the hands of a neighboring club. Delay also hamstrings the Nationals' ability to invest in stadium and related improvements which would generate additional income and help keep the Nationals competitive. In other words, MASN's refusal to pay the fair market value fees required under the contract forces the Nationals either to have to borrow more money to fund cash flow needs (which comes with its own costs) or to limit or to forego the sorts of investments the Nationals should be making to build the club's business for the future."

The Nationals' lawyers argued that the Orioles' arguments were effectively a request for a stay of the judge's order to return to RSDC arbitration that was unjustified, and was undertaken "primarily for the purpose of delay."

How Will the Court Decision Affect the Baltimore Orioles Club and Its Owners?

Peter Angelos has no logical incentive to disrupt how Major League Baseball currently conducts its business. He objected bitterly (and alone among the MLB owners), however, to the 2005 relocation of the Montreal Expos to a city forty miles from his own location.

Notwithstanding this intrusion into the Orioles' baseball neighborhood by another MLB club, the arrival of the Washington Nationals in the Orioles' backyard coincided with a revival of the Orioles' financial and on-field success. After fourteen consecutive losing seasons from 1998 to 2011, the Orioles achieved consecutive winning seasons from 2012 to 2014. The team finished at .500 in 2015.

Home attendance at Orioles games declined from 2,624,740 in 2005 to 1,733,018 in 2010. Home attendance rebounded to 2,464,473 in 2014, before declining to 2,320,590 in 2015. These variations in home attendance might reflect the new competition for fans from the Washington Nationals. They might also reflect the won/loss record of the Orioles.

The 2015 Baltimore riots might also have discouraged some fans from attending games in that season. The riots created the unique spectacle of a home day game played on April 29, 2015 with the gates locked to any fans who might have desired to watch it in person. The Orioles defeated the Chicago White Sox 8-2.

As the saying goes "correlation is not causation." It is difficult to identify the definitive reasons for the Orioles' recent successes. Skillful front office and managerial staffing has contributed to it. Increased cash flow from the increased value of Peter Angelos's majority ownership of MASN, the only MLB club regional sports channel cablecasting the games of two MLB clubs, might also be a factor. The value of the cross-ownership of the Orioles and of MASN has, by some estimates, increased the total market value of the Orioles and MASN by $500 million since 2005 to more than $1 billion in 2015. By comparison, the Nationals' MASN ownership share only contributed about $100 million to their club's total market value.

It can be argued that the 2005 relocation of the Expos franchise to the Orioles neighborhood had a salutary effect on the Orioles' baseball and financial fortunes. This happened not in spite of the increased competition for baseball fans and talent (and that Peter Angelos feared), but exactly *because* of that increased competition.

Monopolies and cartel members have less incentive to innovate, to experiment or to risk their capital in adventurous projects than other businesses that operate in competitive markets. (MLB Advanced Media is not an exception to this rule, if its competition is viewed as coming from other entertainment sources, rather than other baseball leagues.)

Washington, D.C. was excluded from MLB far beyond the expiration date of spurious arguments that it was "not a baseball town". Concurrently, the Orioles endured on-field mediocrity while they were the unchallenged monopolists of major league baseball from Pennsylvania to North Carolina. Once the Orioles faced competition for the attention of regional baseball fans, the club rose to the challenge by improving its on-field performance.

What lessons might Peter Angelos and the Orioles learn from their experience with the 2005 Television Contract that has generously funded the Orioles' revival from 2005 to 2015? The 2014 MLB arbitration award, and Judge Marks's decision vacating it, might leave MASN and the Orioles with only a Pyrrhic victory.

Contracts are a method by which two or more parties allocate the risks and rewards of their economic activities. Peter Angelos sought to "lock-in" a permanent advantage over the future Nationals owners through his majority ownership of the MASN regional sports cable channel.

The five-year rights fees reset procedure in the MASN contract, however, regularly rebalances the relative advantages of MASN ownership against the advantages of club owners' rights to fees for the cablecast of their games. This market-based re-allocation of contract benefits reduces the future profits that MASN owners can expect, because they are diminished by rising rights fees payments. Peter Angelos's argument that he has a right to a guaranteed 20% profit margin for his MASN investment might be a belated recognition that this rights fees re-allocation mechanism will provide him with diminishing future benefits. The pursuit of a sale of MASN to Comcast from 2012 to 2014 might also have been motivated by the diminishing benefits of MASN ownership.

When the next MLB arbitration panel (as is likely) awards rights fees to the Nationals according to the same general methodology used by the 2012 MLB panel, the value of the Orioles' ownership of MASN will decline as the profitability of MASN declines. The fruits of monopolization can be fleeting in any era. In a technologically disruptive era such as our own, the periods of fruitful monopolization shrink further.

The Orioles' best strategy for continued success is to apply the skillful management of talent that has brought them past and current success. They should embrace competition from the Washington Nationals on the field of play, and at the box office, as a spur to their efforts.

How Will the Court's Decision Affect Major League Baseball?

The likely recurring scenario of MASN arbitrations, arbitration awards, and court appeals stretching into an infinite future indicates why Commissioner Bud Selig tried from 2012 to 2014 to broker the sale of the MASN cable channel to the Comcast cable giant. Maybe Commissioner Selig believed that he had made the best compromise he could make, by trading the Nationals' regional cablecast rights to the majority Orioles-owned cable channel in 2005, in return for Peter Angelos's promise to not sue MLB over the Expos' relocation.

Selig satisfied the Major League Baseball Players Association by preserving two franchises that were close to extinction (the Minnesota Twins and the Montreal Expos), thereby preserving fifty to eighty major league jobs for players union members.

Selig transferred the ownership of the near-bankrupt Expos from Jeffrey Loria. It went first to the thirty MLB club owners collectively, and then to the deep pockets of a Washington real estate developer billionaire, Theodore Lerner, and his close-knit family.

Finally, Selig thought he had avoided a lawsuit by Peter Angelos, the owner of the Baltimore Orioles, and a successful class action litigator, against publicity-sensitive MLB. A lawsuit by Peter Angelos against MLB was not avoided, however, but was only postponed from 2005 to 2014.

The uniquely broad antitrust exemption of Major League Baseball was granted by the U.S. Supreme Court in 1922, and was re-affirmed subsequently by the Court and by the U.S. Congress. The Court's later admission that its original rationale for the exemption was wrong – namely that professional baseball was not a business in interstate commerce, and therefore it was not subject to federal or state antitrust laws - has not diminished the exemption's continued vitality.

This is because the exemption has been kept alive, as Oliver Wendell Holmes might have said, "not from logic, but from experience." The most important experience keeping the MLB antitrust exemption alive is the experience that officials elected to political office are more committed to the happiness of their own constituents, as baseball fans, than they are committed to the abstract principle of "Equal Justice Under Law", at least as it applies to baseball.

MLB can dangle possible club franchises before the baseball-hungry eyes of voters somewhere, who otherwise might be inclined to object to MLB's antitrust exemption. MLB can support the relocation of clubs that might feel insufficiently appreciated, either legislatively by anti-exemption legislators, or economically by city and state officials who oppose public financing of stadiums.

All signs would appear to favor MLB and its club owners in continuing their national pastime cartel. The threat of competition from rival leagues has been practically non-existent since the MLB-induced demise of the Mexican League in the 1940s, and since the expiration of the last of the surviving Negro Leagues in the early 1950s.

Immigration laws were eased under the presidency of George W. Bush (a former Texas Rangers club owner) to permit the continued flow of baseball talent from other nations into MLB, and into the minor leagues that MLB mostly controls. The Curt Flood Act established in federal law the free agency rights of major league players, but only as an exception to MLB's continuing antitrust exemption.

Under the relatively enlightened leadership of Commissioner Selig, MLB has wisely avoided labor strikes since 1994, through collective bargaining agreements that reward veteran players, while not unduly squeezing the economic prospects of younger players. (True free agency is limited, however, by these union labor agreements.)

Revenue-sharing of attendance and television revenues under voluntary agreements among MLB clubs has increased on-field competition among big-city and small-city clubs during the past twenty seasons. Commissioner Selig saw the benefits of NFL salary caps, and persuaded owners and players to accept a similar "luxury tax" on the highest club payrolls that indirectly benefits smaller-city clubs.

With little notice by journalists, MLB Advanced Media pioneered internet live-streaming technology through its online presentations of multiple simultaneous baseball games. This 21st century digital venture now provides MLB with a large and growing source of revenue. It has diversified its production into live-streamed programming for other sports clients, and for filmed entertainment providers, such as Netflix and HBO.

Goliath was brought low, however, by one well-aimed shot from a sling. Might Peter Angelos have such a sling?

The Non-Compete Agreement is Becoming the "Reserve Clause" for American Employees

Professional baseball players in the United States were once prohibited from leaving their employers (without permission) under any circumstances in order to compete against them by joining another team. This contract rule was enforced from 1879, when the National League first created the "reserve clause" rule, until 1998 when Congress passed the "Curt Flood Act", which stated that

"Major league baseball players will have the same rights under the antitrust laws as do other professional athletes...."

The reserve clause was enforced by state contract law, and was sanctioned by the unique antitrust exemption granted by the U.S. Supreme Court to professional baseball in 1922. This book offers arguments why baseball's antitrust exemption is harmful to the sport and to the business of baseball. The baseball antitrust exemption, and its related effects, also create a bad model of business behavior for other American businesses.

Although the reserve clause is now history, the Curt Flood Act was written to ensure that all other aspects of professional baseball's antitrust exemption, such as franchise relocation rules, live on. The rise and fall of the baseball reserve clause resembles the increasing use of employee non-compete agreements by American businesses.

The contract law of most states has always allowed certain private employees to be restricted by contract from leaving their employers to compete against them. Agreements to restrict business competition by former employees conflict, however, with the pro-competition goals of American antitrust law and with other public policies. They have only been permitted if these employee restrictions meet certain legal tests.

First, an employee non-compete agreement must be written in an employment contract rather than in a "naked" agreement that simply pays an unrelated worker, who is not an employee, for not competing against a specific business. The interests of a business in protecting its business information, and its investment in employee training, are seen as legitimate purposes for a non-compete agreement.

Second, the non-compete agreement must be "reasonable" in terms of the scope of activities that are restricted, the scope of geographic area covered by the restrictions, and the length of time during which the restriction applies.

For example, state contract law sometimes prohibits the enforcement of non-compete agreements against doctors and lawyers. The availability of doctors to provide critical medical care is usually seen as more important than the competitive interests of a business that employs them. Judges and state legislatures generally believe that the independent judgment of lawyers is necessary for the benefit of clients. It would be compromised by a lawyer's non-compete agreement with his or her former employer, and is usually prohibited.

The level of importance of employee knowledge that justifies a non-compete agreement has recently been drastically reduced. For many years, "non-competes" were only included in the employment contracts, or employee handbooks, of employees with technical and scientific skills. In the past decade, however, they have proliferated into the contracts of summer camp counselors, hairdressers, fast food delivery workers, and journalists.

Any non-compete agreement can be challenged in court as being unreasonable regarding the scope of the employee activities covered by it, the length of time during which it applies, and the geographic scope of its application. Few employees have the time or money, however, to litigate against a former employer who decides to enforce a non-compete agreement.

Three states have never enforced employee non-compete agreements – California, North Dakota and Oklahoma. These states have decided that agreements requiring employees to not divulge or use confidential information and trade secrets acquired during their employment serve the same purposes.

Several recent economic studies indicate that California has gained a significant advantage over other states by not enforcing non-compete agreements in its courts. It has attracted engineers fleeing the enforcement of non-compete agreements in other states. One study indicated that the State of Michigan suffered a decline in entrepreneurship soon after it (unintentionally) eliminated its ban on enforcement of employee non-compete agreements that had existed from 1905 to 1985.

Several states, including Massachusetts, Minnesota and Virginia are considering adopting their own bans on the enforcement of employee non-compete agreements. Employee representatives and venture capital funders have been the strongest advocates for these reforms.

It required almost 120 years for the baseball reserve clause to meet its demise. Perhaps, the far more common "employee reserve clause" will soon follow it into the "dustbin of history".

The Future of Mandatory Arbitration of Business, Employment and Consumer Disputes in the American Economy

A central element of the story of the lawsuit between the Orioles and the Nationals involves another feature of American law that is increasingly controversial. This is the use of mandatory arbitration clauses in business, employee and consumer contracts.

The history of, and the advantages and disadvantages of, arbitration were described in Chapter 6. The related issue of class action litigation, and the ability of businesses to prevent it through mandatory arbitration contract clauses, is also discussed there.

In recent years, the U.S. Supreme Court has restricted the few exceptions that allow the circumvention of these mandatory arbitration contract clauses. In 2010, the "Dodd-Frank Wall

Street Reform and Consumer Protection Act" was passed by Congress. One of its major consumer reform initiatives was the assignment to the newly-created Consumer Financial Protection Bureau of the task of studying the effects of mandatory arbitration contract clauses on consumers of financial products and services.

The CFPB was also given the power to create regulations addressing any negative effects of such clauses. In October 2015, the CFPB issued proposed rules that would "make it illegal for contracts for many types of consumer financial products to have an arbitration clause that deprives consumers of the opportunity to participate in a class action lawsuit."

Whether mandatory arbitrations imposed on consumers, businesses and employees continue to increase will be revealed in the future. The lawsuit of the Orioles against the Nationals and MLB has drawn back the curtain on how one voluntary arbitration proceeding was viewed from vastly different perspectives by two very wealthy professional sports clubs. This story might contain lessons for how mandatory arbitration proceedings will be viewed from the perspective of average businesses, employees and consumers.

The Future of Baseball

The business of baseball is thriving. The game of baseball, however, is at risk of disappearing from the everyday life of Americans. The long-term shift from a rural, agrarian and blue-collar population to an urban, college-educated population accelerates the decline in interest of American youth in the slow and self-effacing game of baseball.

The games of football and basketball are fast and flashy in comparison. Baseball also ideally requires a community of at least eighteen players in order to play it, and a specialized field and equipment. Football and basketball, at a minimum, only require a few players, a ball, and a ten-foot hoop for basketball.

The skills required to play baseball well are subtle and require instruction and repetition. Fathers, or father-figures, have traditionally instructed young players in these skills. Their absence afflicts many low-income communities in many ways, including less baseball-playing.

Finally, why (besides dreams of big-league money) would any parent encourage their multi-talented athletic sons (or daughters) to play baseball in high school? College baseball programs can only offer 11.7 college scholarships to twenty-five players on a baseball team, compared to 85 scholarships on a Division I football team. The below minimum wage salaries paid to minor league baseball players who do not play for college baseball teams is an unattractive alternative for all but the most committed (or desperate) big league aspirants.

Those aspirations start earlier in life than ever before for many players. The most-talented young players, like Bryce Harper, are plucked away from scholastic teams to play on traveling teams of all-stars. Like basketball A.A.U. teams, their primary purpose is to showcase their talent for professional talent scouts. The drain of these players away from scholastic teams reduces the interest of less-talented amateur players in the game of baseball, and erodes their competitive baseball skills.

The current popularity of professional baseball depends on a fan base that is an average of fifty-three years of age. This is about the same average age as for fans of opera. It compares to an average fan age of forty-seven years old for professional football, and thirty-seven years old for professional basketball.

Women, minorities, and lower-income people are less likely to be interested in baseball than men, majority ethnic group members, and higher-income people. While the number of foreign players has increased, the percentage of African-Americans has declined, from nineteen percent of MLB players in 1986, to eight percent in 2014.

The drive for cartel profits has led MLB to focus on building a cheap labor force of Latin American players with work visas as a replacement for American-born baseball players. Foreign players currently make up approximately forty percent of minor league players and one quarter of MLB players. The elimination of major league competitors through MLB's monopolistic practices has shrunk the potential pool of outlets for baseball talent, reducing the popularity of community and informal leagues.

Monopoly profits attract the attention of disruptors who are eager to gain a share of those profits. The list of allies willing to protect monopoly power is usually shorter than the list of potential competitors eager to challenge it.

Business competition can only be addressed successfully for the long term through continuous commitment to excellence, and constant reinvention in order to satisfy constantly changing customer needs and desires. All barriers-to-entry of established businesses against potential competitors are eventually breached.

Major League Baseball has profited from relatively enlightened leadership by its owners and Commissioners since the 1994 players' strike. In order to continue to thrive and to provide the benefits of baseball to large and small communities across the nation and the world, it should not rely on its politically-granted antitrust exemption for its identity and its ethos.

The antitrust exemption can disappear with any vote in Congress. MLB should trust in its innovative abilities to improve the game of baseball, to compete with all forms of entertainment, to spread baseball's health and character-building benefits to all youth, and to preserve the vitality of an old game for the ever-changing future.

ABOUT THE AUTHOR

Charles H. Martin is an attorney with more than twenty years of experience practicing law for private, government and corporate clients. He has taught as a full-time professor of contracts, sales law and international law at U.S. and foreign law schools and universities. He lives in Washington, D.C.

After graduating cum laude from Harvard College, he received his Juris Doctor degree from the University of California (Boalt Hall) School of Law, and his M.B.A. from Columbia Business School. In addition to *Lawyerball*, he is the author of *Every1's Guide to Electronic Contracts*. For more information, see www.charleshmartin.com and www.every1sguide.com.

BIBLIOGRAPHY

ARTICLES

Arcella, Craig F. "Major League Baseball's Disempowered Commissioner: Judicial Ramifications of the 1994 Restructuring." *Columbia Law Review*, Vol. 97, No.8 (Dec., 1997), pp. 2420-2469

Bielski, John R. "Minor League Players Sue MLB for Wage, Antitrust Violations." *The Legal Intelligencer*, June 30, 2015.

Bloomberg Visual Data. "Major League Baseball Franchise Valuations."(with regional sports network and MLB Advanced Media ownership share values) *Bloomberg.com*, October 23, 2013. http://www.bloomberg.com/infographics/2013-10-23/mlb-team-values.html

Brown, Maury. "Major League Baseball Sees Record $9 Billion In Revenues For 2014." *Forbes.com*, December 10, 2014. http://www.forbes.com/sites/maurybrown/2014/12/10/major-league-baseball-sees-record-9-billion-in-revenues-for-2014/

Brown, Maury. "MLB's Billion Dollar TV Deals,

Free Agency, And Why Robinson Cano's Deal With The Mariners Isn't "Crazy"." *Forbes.com*, January 7, 2014. http://www.forbes.com/sites/maurybrown/2014/01/07/mlbs-billion-dollar-tv-deals-free-agency-and-why-robinson-canos-deal-with-the-mariners-isnt-crazy/#2715e4857a0b33e5b8c4e267

Brown, Maury. "MLB National Television Contract Details." *The Biz of Baseball*, October 2, 2012. http://bizofbaseball.com/index.php?option=com_content&view=article&id=5734&Itemid=203

Brustein, Joshua. "Why HBO, Netflix, and Amazon Want Your Kids." *Bloomberg.com*, August 14, 2015. http://www.bloomberg.com/news/articles/2015-08-14/why-hbo-netflix-and-amazon-want-your-kids

Carleton, Barney. "MLB Teams Capitalize on Local Television Rights." *Upper Deck Chatter*, January 4, 2014. https://upperdeckchatter.wordpress.com/2014/01/04/mlb-teams-capitalize-on-local-television-rights/

Casavell, AJ, and Paul Casella. "MLB Organizational Report Cards." *Sports on Earth*, December 15, 2015. http://www.sportsonearth.com/article/159673174/mlb-team-report-cards

Davis, Noah and Lopez, Michael. "Don't Be Fooled By Baseball's Small-Budget Success Stories." *FiveThirtyEightSports*, July 8, 2015. http://fivethirtyeight.com/features/dont-be-fooled-by-baseballs-small-budget-success-stories/

Dokoupil, Tony. "Does Major League Baseball Exploit Latin Players?" *NBCnews.com*, October 21, 2014. http://www.nbcnews.com/news/latino/does-major-league-baseball-exploit-latino-players-n228316

Dosh, Kristi. " MLB's Revenue-Sharing and the Luxury Tax Are Not One in the Same." *The Biz of Baseball*, January 27, 2012. http://www.kristidosh.com/wp-content/uploads/2012/01/Dosh_-MLBs-Revenue-Sharing-and-the Luxury-Tax-Are-Not-One-in-the-Same-Biz-of-Baseball-4-19 10.pdf

Fisher, Marc. "Baseball is struggling to hook kids –

and risks losing fans to other sports." *The Washington Post*, April 5, 2015.

Flint, Joe. "Resistance to Dodgers Channel Sends Message on Pricing." *Wall Street Journal*, September 29, 2014.

Goldberg, Eric. "New proposal to ban companies from using arbitration clauses as a free pass to avoid accountability." *Consumer Financial Protection Bureau Blog*, October 7, 2015. http://www.consumerfinance.gov/blog/new-proposal-to-ban-companies-from-using-arbitration-clauses-as-a-free-pass-to-avoid-accountability/

Gordon, Ian. "Inside Major League Baseball's Dominican Sweatshop System." *Mother Jones*, March/April 2013. http://www.motherjones.com/politics/2013/03/baseball-dominican-system-yewri-guillen

Haupert, Michael J. "The Economic History of Major League Baseball". *EH.Net Encyclopedia*, edited by Robert Whaples. December 3, 2007. http://eh.net/encyclopedia/the-economic-history-of-major-league-baseball/

Hoffman, Shawn. "The Enigma That is MLB

Network", *Baseball Prospectus*, May 20, 2010. http://www.baseballprospectus.com/article.php?articleid=10922

Jaffe, Harry. "Ted Lerner Plays Ball." *Washingtonian*, June 1, 2007. http://www.washingtonian.com/2007/06/01/ted-lerner-plays-ball/

Johnson, Martin. "The Royals Are the Epitome of a Moneyball Team." *Slate.com*, October 27, 2015. http://www.slate.com/articles/sports/sports_nut/2015/10/why_the_kansas_city_royals_are_actually_the_perfect_moneyball_team.html

Justice, Richard. "Manfred proud of MLB's advancing technology." *MLB.com News*, January 7, 2016. http://m.mlb.com/news/article/161295380/rob-manfred-discusses-baseballs-technology

McMillan, Robert, and King, Rachel. "Netflix to Pull Plug on Final Data Center." *The Wall Street Journal*, August 13, 2015.

Nagel, Mark S., Brown, Matt T., Rascher, Daniel A., McEvoy, Chad D. "Major League Baseball Anti-Trust Immunity: Examining the Legal and Financial Implications of Relocation Rules."

Entertainment and Sports Law Journal, January 2007, Volume 4, Number 3.

Orinick, Steve. "MLB Team Payrolls 1998-2015." *Steve O's Baseball Umpire Resources*, http://www.stevetheump.com/Payrolls.htm

Ozanian, Mike. "MLB Worth $36 Billion As Team Values Hit Record $1.2 Billion Average." Forbes.com, March 25, 2015. http://www.forbes.com/sites/mikeozanian/2015/03/25/mlb-worth-36-billion-as-team-values-hit-record-1-2-billion-average/#2715e4857a0b5914992a741e

Pappas, Doug. "Inside the Major League Rules." *Outside the Lines*, Fall 2002 Society for American Baseball Research (SABR) Business of Baseball Committee Newsletter. http://roadsidephotos.sabr.org/baseball/02-4rules.htm

Pilon, Mary. "Are Minor Leaguers Paid Legal Wages?", *The New Yorker*, August 20, 2015. http://www.newyorker.com/news/sporting-scene/are-minor-leaguers-paid-legal-wages

Popper, Ben. "The Changeup – How baseball's tech team built the future of television." *The Verge*,

August 4, 2015. http://www.theverge.com/2015/8/4/9090897/mlb-bam-live-streaming-internet-tv-nhl-hbo-now-espn

Rubenfeld, Samuel. "MLB Policy Changes Make Cuban Baseball Players Free Agents in U.S." *Wall Street Journal*, February 4, 2015.

Schoenfeld, Bruce. "Baltimore's Blue Collar Boss, The complicated Peter Angelos." *Sports Business Journal*, August 26, 2013. http://www.sportsbusinessdaily.com/Journal/Issues/2013/08/26/Franchises/Peter-Angelos.aspx

Schoenfield, David. "Still 30 teams: Contraction timeline." *ESPN.com*, February 5, 2002. http://assets.espn.go.com/mlb/s/2002/0205/1323230.html

Schwartz, Peter J. "Yankees Among 10 MLB Teams Valued at More Than $1 Billion." *Bloomberg.com*, October 23, 2013. http://www.bloomberg.com/news/articles/2013-10-23/yankees-among-10-mlb-teams-valued-at-more-than-1-billion

Steinberg, Sid. "MLB Strikes Out Seeking Minor-

League Wage-and-Hour Suit Dismissal." *The Legal Intelligencer*, November 11, 2015. http://bit.ly/1S4udby

Thompson, Derek. "Which Sports Have the Whitest/Richest/Oldest Fans?" *The Atlantic*, February 10, 2014. http://www.theatlantic.com/business/archive/2014/02/which-sports-have-the-whitest-richest-oldest-fans/283626/

Urmacher, Kevin. "Baseball's decline in America.", *The Washington Post*, April 5, 2015. https://www.washingtonpost.com/national/baseballs-decline-in-america/2015/04/05/a18bce94-dbee-11e4-a500-1c5bb1d8ff6a_graphic.html

Wagner, James. "MLB is addressing a need with Spanish language interpreters." *The Washington Post*, January 14, 2016. https://www.washingtonpost.com/news/nationals-journal/wp/2016/01/14/mlb-is-addressing-a-need-with-spanish-language-interpreters/

Walker, Childs. "Peter Angelos remains a powerful paradox." *The Baltimore Sun*, October 2, 2010. http://articles.baltimoresun.com/2010-10-02/news/bs-md-angelos-20101002_1_peter-angelos-orioles-owner-the-orioles

REPORTS

Neilsen – <u>Year in Sports Media Report 2014</u>. http://www.nielsen.com/us/en/insights/reports/2015/the-year-in-sports-media-report-2014.html

BOOKS

Frommer, Frederic J. *You Gotta Have Heart, A History of Washington Baseball from 1859 to the 2012 National League East Champions*. Lanham, Maryland: Taylor Trade Publishing, 2013.

Lewis, Michael. *Moneyball, The Art of Winning an Unfair Game*. New York, NY: W.W. Norton & Company, Inc., 2004.

Pessah, Jon. *The Game, Inside the Secret World of Major League Baseball's Power Brokers*. New York, NY: Little, Brown and Company, 2015.

Ruck, Rob. *Raceball, How the Major Leagues Colonized the Black and Latin Game*. Boston, MA: Beacon Press, 2012.

Wallop, Douglass. *The Year The Yankees Lost The*

Pennant. New York, NY: W.W. Norton & Company, Inc., 2004.

Made in the USA
Middletown, DE
22 April 2016